A Woman's Love Is Never Good Enough

Second Edition

Charlena E. Jackson, B.S., M.S., M.H.A

Printed in the United States of America
2nd edition, October, 2019
ISBN: 978-1-7340704-2-2

Books by Charlena E. Jackson, B.S., M.S., M.H.A

No Cross, No Crown: Trust God Through the Battle
No Cross, No Crown: Trust God Through the Battle 2nd edition
I'm Speaking Up but You're Not Listening
I'm Speaking Up but You're Not Listening 2nd edition
Teachers Just Don't Understand Bullying Hurts
Teachers Just Don't Understand Bullying Hurts 2nd edition
A Woman's Love is Never Good Enough
A Woman's Love is Never Good Enough 2nd Edition
Unapologetic for My Flaws and All
Unapologetic for My Flaws and All 2nd edition
Dying on the Inside and Suffocating on the Outside
Dear Fathers of the Fatherless Children

To:

My precious, beautiful, wonderful, and loving daughter, Sarah. Life is beautiful; enjoy everything it has to offer with love, peace, joy, and happiness! I love you so much – words cannot describe how I feel. I am so blessed to have you as my daughter!

My mother, Mae Jackson. You are the definition of a Trailblazer. You are the ripple effect of hope and determination. I love you dearly!

My sister, Jawauna, we've known each other for three decades. Our bond will always be unbreakable. Sis, we've been through a lot together; I am so blessed to have you in my life! I am beyond grateful for your unconditional love and support! I will always love you unto the moon and back!

My sissy, Ashley, I am so thankful for our sisterhood. It has bloomed into a beautiful garden of flowers. Thank you so much for listening to all of my long voice recordings and for giving the best advice! Thank you for always being here for me. You've been such a blessing in my life—more than you would ever know. Thank you for your love and support! You are the best! I love you so much!

My big sis, Tenisha. When I am having a challenging day, your laughter will always take away my worries. We have to much fun together. I love our sister-talk. When we spend time together our problems melt away. You are such a joy and a bundle of love! I have so much love for you!

Kim, although we do not talk as often, you will always be my sister. We've had so many ups and downs. I miss us cracking funny jokes and having a good laugh when nobody else understood. I want to apologize for not being there when you needed me the most. Thank you so much for all of your love and support. Your actions spoke louder than your words. I will always love you.

Contents

Love.

What is love? It is the essence of the unknown and will overwhelm you if you do not realize you are giving too much of yourself.

Love is an intense emotion that will take a toll on you mentally, emotionally and physically in an unselfish, yet bittersweet way that develops into a deep affection; and sometimes, an unknown outcome.

Love is filled with a lot of sacrifices and resentment and is underestimated in so many ways. It is something of a Catch-22 and an overwhelming source of empowerment. You might feel as though love didn't give you an answer to the questions that you asked. You've been waiting for days, even years; and perhaps you will never receive an answer at all. Maybe you've received an answer; however, it wasn't what you expected. The question is—did you accept the answer, or are you still searching for the answer you desire?

Love is a strange word. It can be misleading and confusing. It can break you down with tender grace and mercy, while at the same time building you up to become a powerful force—and after that, you will never be the same.

The ripple effects of love are beautiful and peaceful, yet can also be disturbing and ruthless. At times, love takes advantage of its powers; it causes you to suffer from loving someone too much and finding yourself lost, without hope and giving too much of yourself to the point that you suffer because you're neglecting yourself. It can cause you to lose faith. Its tremendous effect has a full impact as you find peace and happiness in your life.

Love will open your eyes to realize you are not the victim; instead, you are victorious over the trials, battles, and challenges of life.

Love will show you that you do not have to search for it because it abides in you whole-heartedly. Love can be bittersweet but its grace is patience. Love is difficult but its mercy is tender. At times love might make you feel empty but you are never alone.

Love abounds against all odds. One thing about love is that it comes with many sacrifices. Its good intentions always reassure you that in order to love someone else, you must be willing to love yourself first.

Pioneers

A woman is a visionary. She gathers great strength through the hardest challenges. She suits up for the battles that are set before her and executes them without hesitation.

A woman always gives away the heart of her soul; to her husband and/or significant other, children, family, friends, and in the workplace. A woman goes through so much emotionally, physically, and mentally. However, most of the time it goes unnoticed.

As a little girl, a woman is groomed to become a wife and a mother. She is trained to always make wise decisions, yet there will forever be limits and boundaries. As I look back, I remember being told what I could and could not do, simply because I was a girl.

A little girl is told she cannot act like a boy; if she does, she will be classified as a "tomboy." Climbing trees was prohibited, instead, she was taught to put a baby doll in a stroller and take the doll for a walk. She couldn't sit as she pleased; she was told to only sit with her ankles crossed.

Girls were given a kitchen playset that was equipped with a stove, sink, and an accessory set of play food dishes, pots and pans, etc., along with a tea set to bring out the "elegance" in them. As the saying goes, "Girls are sugar and spice, and everything nice."

I'm taken aback by how girls are groomed to be a certain way; however, boys are able to love life and live freely without limitations and criticism.

I was raised by both of my parents, my grandparents, aunts, and uncles. I was blessed because I had the best of both worlds. My grandparents were very active in my life. My siblings and I lived next door to my grandparents (my mother's parents). My grandmother was a stay-at-home mom and grandmother. I remember when I was in elementary school, I had to write a paper about my hero. I wrote a paper on my grandmother because she was, and still, is my Shero.

My grandmother was the foundation of the household, and she kept it together. She cooked, cleaned, prepared my granddaddy's clothes for the next day for work, his lunch, etc. I always thought my grandmother was a "superwoman." She faithfully had breakfast, snack, lunch, snack, dinner, and snack prepared for us daily.

When my siblings and I were sick, we used to pack our clothes, and roll our suitcases across the driveway to our grandmother's house. We always wanted our grandparents to take care of us. There is something about grandparents' love that makes a child feel secure, loved, and precious.

When my parents were at work, we would stay with my grandparents until they arrived home. Within that time, most days, my granddaddy would pick us up from elementary school. He always took off his hat and opened and closed the car door for his granddaughters. He taught my sisters and me to always wait for a man to open the door; because we are queens, we are beautiful, we are loved, and worthy of respect.

My grandparents and parents taught my sisters and me that women are equal. My siblings and I had a kitchen and tea set, baby dolls and strollers, too. We played with them a lot. However, most of the time, we were either playing with my cousins, climbing trees, and going on imaginary treasure hunts. Instead of playing on the swing set we would climb up on it, pretending to get away from the "bad guys."

Every day, my parents and grandparent told my sisters and I that we were beautiful. My mother made sure we looked like little girls; our hair always was done, and we wore sundresses every now and then, but my sisters and I always wanted to wear tennis shoes and pants. However, regardless of what we wore, my mother made sure we dressed the part and were always pretty.

My daddy and granddaddy always groomed my sister and me how to think like a man and act like a lady. When I was in fifth grade my friends and I were playing on the playground and a teacher said, "A little girl is supposed to act ladylike. She should sit down, look pretty, cross her legs, and keep her head in a book. As she ages and becomes a woman, she will be taught how to be an obedient wife and raise a family."

I talked to my granddaddy about it when he picked me up from school; he said, "Lena, you wake up pretty every morning. You can do some things a little boy can do, and as you get older, if you put your mind to it, you will be able to do anything a man can do—and better. Don't ever let anyone get in your head to make you think otherwise." I smiled, and from that day forth I was an unstoppable and fearless little girl.

As I watched my grandmother prepare the dough to make her famous homemade butter biscuits; she walked to the oven to check on her one-of-a-kind pound cake. When her cakes were in the oven, we had to tiptoe around the house. At times, we would whisper because we didn't want the cakes to "fall."

My grandmother knew something was bothering me. She asked, "Child, what is wrong with you? You are deep in thought. What's on your mind?"

I didn't know how to talk to my grandmother about what the teacher said to me on the playground because my grandmother fit the description of a lady the teacher had told us about. "It's nothing important," I answered.

She smoothed the dough with a rolling pin and said, "Yes, it is. What is it, child?"

"Grandma, seriously, it's not important," I answered, as I pinched the dough with my fingers.

My grandmother picked up the round cookie cutter and said, "Help me cut out the dough."

As I started to form the cookie dough into perfect circles, I told my grandmother what my teacher had said. I went on to say, "Grandma, I didn't know how to talk to you about it because all the things she said a woman should do, you do them for granddaddy and for us. I didn't want to hurt your feelings, and I didn't want you to think I didn't want to be like you, or I was ashamed, because I'm not," I said with excitement, "You are my Shero!"

My grandmother smiled as she brushed butter on the biscuits and said,

"My sweet baby girl, we all have a choice in life. I always wanted to be a singer, but I decided to get married at an early age, have children, and take care of your granddaddy. That was my choice. If you do not remember anything else I tell you, remember, you always have a choice and freedom of speech. You've had a lot of warriors who put their lives on the line so that women could be treated equally to men. What your teacher told you today isn't your life if you do not want it to be. Again, you have a choice."

My grandmother gently curved her hand and put it on my cheek and said, "I know you are not ashamed of me, and I know I am your Shero. How can I forget? You tell me every day. I want you to know I love taking care of my family; it gives me great joy! Although I wanted to be a singer, I sing every day. I sing in the tub, I sing while I clean, cook, iron clothes, and I sing to the good Lord every chance I can get; and He listens. When my children were carrying my grandchildren, I sang to them, and I sing to all my grandbabies. My dreams weren't shattered. I am living my dreams, I'm here for my family and I wouldn't have it any other way."

I smiled and said, "Grandma, this is why you are my shero."

My grandmother looked me in the eyes and said, "Do not let anyone tell you what you can and cannot do. You are a smart little girl who will turn into a trailblazing woman with a mind of your own, will speak your piece, walk with your head up, and with your shoulders wide."

I laughed and said, "Wow, Grandma, you described yourself, because you are superwoman."

My grandmother had a good laugh and replied, "I am a woman who knows when, where, and how to speak up. Just because I stay home and take care of my family and the house doesn't mean that I'm invisible. I am a driving force; and a powerful one at that. I am very involved in the church, I help the homeless at the Food Bank, and I am active in my grandchildren's lives. I have everything I want, and more. Always remember to lead by example, because I raised all of my children not to be labeled, but to be powerful like me; and even more powerful. Appreciate what you have and make it work for you."

Although I was young, I understood everything my grandmother told me. Later that evening, I laid back on the couch and enjoyed my grandmother's melodies. When my grandmother sings, her voice sounds like flowing water; so refreshing, soothing, and peaceful. I began to think about how much my grandmother did for the church. She was the Food Bank President—we used to go to the church to help her put boxes together for the sick, shut-ins, and homeless. My grandmother is a prayer warrior—she would wake up every morning at 5 a.m. to read her bible, pray for her family, and then start her pioneer duties.

When my granddaddy couldn't pick us up from school, my grandmother would pick us up or we would catch the bus. If we caught the bus my grandmother would be waiting on the porch for us with hot buttermilk biscuits, warm syrup and refreshing milk. After our tummies were full, she would help us with our homework, and we would help her bake pound cakes and cook dinner.

People at the church looked up to my grandmother; she was also the Missionary President. She and the church members would visit the sick in their homes, nursing homes and hospitals. She would make food for them and their families. Every day people would call my grandmother for prayer, so with that being said, my grandmother lived on the phone, but she managed to get everything done, and so much more.

There were times when my grandmother squeezed in time to go to our parent-teacher conferences because my parents weren't able to make it. My grandmother was very strict, but her love was unconditional in her own unique way.

My daddy is an amazing man. He taught his girls to always speak our minds in a respectful manner. He is a Marine, therefore, my siblings and I were raised differently. We had a lot of rules and regulations in our household. Rules and regulations formed the structure within the family, and the structure formed order, patience, and wisdom.

As a little girl, there weren't limitations or boundaries placed before me. My parents and grandparents taught me that I have a voice and should never settle for less.

My daddy's mother, Grandma Sarah Lee, was a bad mama jama; she spoke her mind at any given place and time. She was a fearless woman, and she would set a person straight in a minute. I felt bad for people who got in her way because she was a force to be reckoned with. Whatever she believed in, she fought for until it was in her favor. One thing was for sure, she didn't take no for an answer. Her drive was like fire meeting gasoline for the first time; there was no coming back from that. I've always admired how she stood her ground because her voice was always heard; whether you wanted to hear it or not.

My Big Momma, who was my daddy's grandmother, was respected on the west side of Atlanta. She taught the girls in our family about the cutthroat meaning of life. She groomed us to prepare and watch out for our enemies. If I learned one thing from her (I learned a lot!) it would be that she always used to say that most of the time your enemy is standing right in your face. She always told us to never let anyone underestimate our character as a woman. She always instilled in us, as women, to never become a prisoner for anyone. A woman should never underestimate her worth and her abilities. To never be afraid to roar and always soar as high as she wants to go because the sky is never the limit.

My grandmother Sarah, my other grandmother on my daddy's side, was so humble. I often wondered, *how could a person be so humble during trying times?* Every time I talked to her about my problems, she would turn a negative situation into a positive outcome. Every time I added more negative fuel to the flame she would always humble her soul and turn our talk into a graceful, peaceful conversation. She always used to say, "My sweet baby girl, prayer and patience is the key."

I didn't understand. She smiled at me in the humblest way and said, "You have to be aware of God's higher power. He has the first and last word; therefore, you shouldn't worry about what men can do to you. What they "think" they can do will turn into dust, and God will blow it away as if it never existed. Stop worrying your sweet little heart, you are too young to stress over something you can't handle. Turn it over to God; He is the only one who can turn crooked roads straight."

I laid my head on her lap and told her I loved her so much because after talking to her I always felt at peace. She rubbed my head and said, "As women, we cannot be afraid to jump; we will land in the Great Divine's hands because He is our safety net. We have to stay humble in our challenging times; that is when we become stronger and wiser.

One thing I do know, we, as women, are creating a masterpiece. Our minds are building a strong foundation so when the boomerang comes back around, we are able to step back, reconnect, rest, and recharge. That is when we have the power to increase our abilities to expand our vision to take flight."

I smiled and laughed slightly. She continued, "Get out of the driver's side and let the Great Divine lead the way and take the wheel. My sweet baby girl, sit on the passenger side, put your hands in the air, and enjoy the ride."

Until this day, I miss my Grandma Sarah. She was so easy to talk to. I felt her love, and I knew I was loved. I think of her often, and I wish she was still here. She is truly missed.

My mother was a wounded warrior who used her scars to give her the turbocharge she needed to make it through another day. She had a rough marriage, and I always believed my mother stayed because she wanted her children to be raised by two parents. My siblings and I witnessed the brutal arguments and physical fights.

Although my mother didn't cry around her children, I saw her pain. I felt her drive, and I absorbed her strategy of how she was silently coming back with the thunder of great strength.

From the outside, I'd witnessed my mother's rough seasons, but I could only imagine what she was going through on the inside. Sometimes silence can be the loneliest place. I noticed that during her silence, my mother was able to collect her thoughts and find herself.

She endured so much hurt and pain, yet she conquered her challenges and made it through another new day. My mother was an expert at working through her silence and making her accomplishments come to life.

After my parents got a divorce when I was in my senior year in high school, my mother was left in a bad place. There were times when she struggled to fly. The sorrow in my mother's eyes was unbearable to see. The load was too much to carry, yet my mother made the best out of what she was given. She completed college, started from the bottom at her place of work and worked her way up to become a Branch Manager.

My mother is a strong woman who is a groundbreaker, a warrior, and a survivor. Through all of the curveballs that she caught, she returned the favor and made a home run. She put her armor on and turned her disappointments into achievements.

I felt as though I followed in my mother's footsteps. I too was left alone to take care of my home. Although, my mother had help here and there from her family, and my siblings and I were older when my parents got a divorce, my children were ten, six, and the youngest only five months old when my husband left. I was a nervous wreck because I had so much on my mind and on my plate.

I am not perfect, and every marriage has its challenges, but I never thought my husband would walk out on his family and never come back. I had my flaws and so did he, but one thing's for sure, I knew I would never leave without notice. I was left in the dark without a spark or flicker of light that the eye could see, but I had a dim light shining within my soul.

Life has a funny way of expressing itself. I learned that during light or darkness we have to trust the path and follow directions in order to survive the transformation.

The darkness wasn't negative energy, it was healing—it balanced my soul. It helped me to trust whatever unfolded and to believe and have faith in what I couldn't see. It prepared me for the battles that I wasn't prepared for. They sneaked up on me and revealed themselves without notice. When obstacles jumped out at me without warning, I knew I wasn't alone. My faith was improving during the darkest hours of my life.

The darkness taught me to trust my intuition. It helped me to coordinate and bring peace within my center when I walked into the unknown. The darkness helped me to know when I needed to surrender and to dissect each circumstance.

Slowly but surely, the darkness revealed light; and as the dim light shine brighter, I was mentally, physically, and emotionally prepared to battle the raging storms and the unfair, distasteful barriers. When my bags were too heavy and weighing me down, the darkness taught me when to put them down and focus on me. It taught me when to let go and know I could not change the situation. Most importantly, the darkness taught me that I could work through my trying times and make the best of what I was given.

Darkness is not a bad place; it depends on how one looks at it. It keeps me from going insane and losing my mind. Darkness rejuvenates my mind, restores peace and teaches me how to pray and ask for help. When we prepare for rest, we want the room to be dark; therefore, we close the blinds, cut off the lights and television, and eliminate any distractions so we can get a peaceful night's rest. Darkness renews your mind. It restores your energy and it gives you the strength you need to get through another day.

Darkness, also, represent truth—I notice there are a lot of people in the world today whose true colors come out in their darkest hours. They are good at hiding in the light because they are afraid the darkness will unveil their fear and who they truly are as a person.

If darkness didn't exist, the stars and the moon wouldn't be able to shine. The stars give me hope; as they shine so brightly, I know my blessings will shine even brighter. Embrace the darkness; it will give you well-needed rest, and as you walk out into the light the sun will complement your renewed strength.

Throughout my difficult challenges, I managed to take advantage of the opportunities that were laid before me. It wasn't always easy, but my struggles gave me the determination to strive and work hard for what I wanted. When I had a major shift in life, I was told over and over again that I had limitations. I felt helpless and hopeless.

There were so many people who were willing to lend a helping hand of negativity, as opposed to giving me encouraging words. I wasn't willing to be limited to boundaries that I knew I could push through. I knew what I wanted, and I was willing to work hard by any means necessary to fight fire with fire. I was always taught that nothing is given—it is earned. I knew if I wanted to conquer my goals, I had to make sacrifices.

Without fail, a woman is always walking into the unknown. It seems as though it is so easy to blame and point the finger at a woman. What others fail to realize is that a woman might not always know what lies ahead of her, but she will always find a way to get through it.

When she hits the ground, she will bounce right back up. The road may twist and turn; there will be a few steep hills and sharp curves, but she will never give up because she is unstoppable.

A woman imagines what she wants, and plans mentally for the transition. She gathers strength to prepare for the emotional challenges in her life that lie ahead. Conflicts try to break her stride but although she is filled with pain, she still walks with confidence, and with a smile on her face.

When there is a world of distractions and difficult decisions to make when a woman finds herself straying off the tracks, she will not feel defeated.

She is courageous!

She is victorious!

She is a pioneer!

AFFIRMATION

*"Wake up! Become more aware and alive of what feeds **YOUR** soul without seeking permission from others. Many curve balls have been thrown. Don't hesitate—NOW is the time to hit a home run."*

Underestimated

I never understood why a woman's strength, character and hard work are underestimated. A woman has to prove herself to be worthy in just about everything she does. When it comes to her relationships such as friendship, marriage, being a mother, daughter, sister, and a co-worker, someone will find fault in what she does because nothing is ever good enough.

One would think friendship is simple and doesn't require much work. A woman's friendship is always judged and her loyalty is always being tested. There have been many "friendships" I had that ended over petty arguments, jealousy, comparison, and competition. There were times when I said the wrong thing and some friends were offended; and vice versa.

During my teenage years, I was the type of person that couldn't accept the truth. I would ask my close friends for advice, and most of the time if it wasn't what I wanted to hear, I would disagree and stop talking to them for a while.

One day, one of my close friends voiced her opinion and told me I did not know when and how to accept the truth. I was offended. A couple of days later, another friend told me the same thing. She said, "Charlena when you ask for advice, I hesitate about whether I should tell you the truth, or lie and tell you what you want to hear because I do not want to lose the friendship we've built."

I then begin to think to myself, *is this true? When someone tells me something I do not want to hear, do I always get offended?*

Believe it or not, a week later another close friend of mine said, "Charlena, I know you might take this the wrong way, but why ask for advice when you do not know how to receive criticism or the truth? Why bother to ask?" She continued and bluntly said, "I prefer that you do not ask me for advice."

I was taken aback because my friends didn't know each other. They went to different schools, but they knew of each other. I kept a poker face; I knew then that I was the problem and I had a serious issue of not wanting to know the truth.

For weeks, it bothered me. I had to finally break down and look at myself in the mirror. I thought to myself, *I wonder how long I've been doing this, and how long have they been feeling this way?* They were tired of overlooking my annoying ways. I had to take ownership of my actions. I sincerely apologized for my habits and I thanked them for pointing them out to me.

I was on a personal mission to change for the better. I had to work on my old 'cycle' until the mission was completed. It wasn't easy. My friends and I were always butting heads. I felt like they were taking advantage of my apology and my willingness to change. However, they weren't. One thing's for sure, change isn't easy.

Change is like pulling the wool from your eyes and seeing the light for the first time. If you are set in your old ways, it takes people who care about you to help you get over as many hurdles as it takes to finish the course.

I had my ups and downs. I felt as though the truth was my enemy because it was so harsh, cold, blunt, and at times unbearable to hear. In the past, lies felt more like angels and music to my ears. The truth felt like demons because it was so merciless.

I was a major 'work in progress.' I appreciate those friends to this day for telling me the truth. I have so much gratitude because they were willing to travel the rugged road with me.

Although I experienced this issue during my teenage years, it taught me a lesson because I do not want someone to lie to me because they feel like I cannot accept the truth, or because it causes stress on them. Most importantly, I do not want to lie to myself thinking what I am saying is real and true while knowing it was a lie the entire time.

As I lived, learned, and became wiser during my adult years, it was funny how karma came back to teach me a lesson to help others. Sometimes it worked in my favor. Most days, it taught me how to leave well enough alone.

A friend from the past had an STD that was contagious, and there wasn't a cure. I told her that before she had sex with the men she was seeing, she needed to be honest with them. She didn't want to hear the truth; she took what I said and left. That destroyed our friendship. Often, I would apologize for telling the truth. It was stressful 'walking on glass' because I had to be cautious of what I said. It wasn't friendship; it was more like being a lifeguard protecting someone's feelings because they did not want to hear the truth.

A friendship shouldn't be a competition. Everyone should be their own individual person with hope, passion, and love to teach and learn from each other. I had a friend who always tried to keep up with me. Everything I wanted to do—she wanted to do it too. It got to the point where I would continue the friendship with her, but I wouldn't tell her my next move. Our friendship faded into the background because we didn't have anything to talk about since she couldn't compare herself to me.

Strangely, I had one friend who always stopped talking to me when she had a new boyfriend. When she was single, she made time for our friendship. However, when she met another guy, the communication would cease. I think we all have a friend like that.

She and I had a lot of disagreements. We argued over why she would only date men who attended church. She acted as though men who attended church were saints; as if they never did anything wrong. Sadly, the men she dated in her church would take her out, but later wanted a nightcap. I never understood her. She would say, men outside of the church are "worldly people." We all have our opinion; however, I can't help but think, *aren't we all "worldly people?"* This took a toll on our friendship, and honestly, we couldn't even agree to disagree. However, that was fine, because some people are meant to come into your life just for a season.

There was a friendship I had where I felt we wanted to switch lives with each other. I had kids. However, she didn't, and at the time, she had freedom and a college education. I didn't. I do believe we were envious of each other's lives, but that never came between our friendship. Although we do not talk often, one thing's for sure we, will always have a sisterhood. As young girls going to middle school together, we had a lot of bittersweet days. We always had each other's back. I must say, she had my back so many times and helped me when I had my first son and my daughter. As of today, we both have what we always yearned for. She has her son and is married, and I have my children, my education and my career.

However, you have some friendships/sisterhoods that are for a lifetime. I have one childhood friend who I call my sister. We went to elementary school through college together. During elementary, we use to walk to and from school together. We were in the same class, and every day after school we would make a snack at her house and complete our homework. We didn't have the same birth parents, but for sure it is undeniable that we are sisters.

We both made the best of what was given to us. There were people who thought we were privileged because of our parents' careers. Little did they know, what was going on inside the walls of our homes. We would share our stories and we were each other's way out of misery.

We most definitely had our ups and downs. There were times when our sisterhood was tested because of misunderstandings, but just like any siblings, we fussed, talked it out and got over it.

One of our biggest arguments would be over something really stupid. Every single morning, on our way to high school she would play *In Due Time* by *Outkast*. It was too early in the morning to listen to her rap and sing. What made it worse was when Cee-Lo Green's part came on! Oh, my goodness. She would get down to the nitty-gritty, singing loud, hard and strong.

> *"Strugglin's just a part of my day*
> *Many obstacles have been placed in my way*
> *I know the only reason that I make it through*

Is because I never stop believing in you
Some people wonder why we here in the first place
They can't believe 'cause they ain't never seen your face
But even when you pray, the next day you gotta try
Can't wait for nobody to come down out the sky
You've got to realize that the world's a test
You can only do your best and let Him do the rest
You've got your life, and got your health
So quit procrastinating and push it yourself
You've got to realize that the world's a test
You can only do your best and let Him do the rest
You've got your life, and got your health
So quit procrastinating..."

In Due Time was played faithfully every single morning until the last day of school during our 12ᵗʰ-grade year.

After we graduated high school; off to college we went. At that time, I had my oldest son. She and I were pregnant together with our girls. We worked together as a team. When we couldn't afford daycare from time to time, we would watch each other's children.

There were times when we only had each other, and we were all each other had. We went through a lot together. We were stereotyped by people we didn't know, including our family and friends, because we had children. We were asked by people, "What do you all think you're doing? Saying you're going to college as if you are going to finish with children stuck to your hips." We learned the hard way that life isn't fair. I am happy to say that during the process we developed thick skin. The best part of it all; our skin was thicker together because we lifted each other up at the right time. We were each other's backbone and rock.

When we both were going through hard times, we were there for each other every waking moment of the day. She and I never ever fueled off each other's struggles. Instead, we helped fuel each other's empty tank with encouraging words, a helping hand, and/or just listening by not saying anything at all.

After all the criticism and life's disappointments, Jawauna and I graduated from college. She graduated a year before I did, but we got through it together. The bond we have will not ever be broken. For three decades and counting, we have been the best of friends; something that money cannot buy.

I met my sissy Ashley in undergraduate school when we were in the same class, Psychology. It was funny because she thought I was a Ms. Goody-two-shoes. Our professor asked us what we ate for breakfast—I raised my hand and said, "Toasted wheat bread with egg white and a small bowl of oatmeal." I forget the question my professor asked, it had something to do with children, but I remember my answer. I offered to be a surrogate for a friend of mine who couldn't have a baby at that given time. Ashley apparently didn't like my answers—she thought I was showing off.

As for me, after class, she and I were walking down the hallway. She was quiet and so humble. I told her she wasn't a "good girl" as she appeared to be. She smiled and then laughed and said, "Okay."

As we got to know each other, we talked and laughed about how we "assume" and "label" each other's character. We've been close friends ever since. As our friendship grew stronger, we became closer and started to call each other sisters. We had our ups and downs too; however, we would talk it over and moved forward.

I was having issues with my ex-husband. He wanted to see the children after he up and left without notice and didn't come back. I was struggling to survive with three children. I had to start over as we were living in the projects because we were kicked out of the comfort of our home.

Nearly two years of picking up the pieces and getting my life back on track, he wanted to give me short notice to come and see the kids. I was upset. He was living the life of a single man; as if he didn't have any responsibility and acting like he didn't do anything wrong. I felt so frustrated about his, *I don't give a shit,* attitude. To be honest, I was a woman scorned.

I asked sissy for advice. She said, "Sis, I think you should let him see the kids."

I honestly disagreed. I was upset and said, "Sis, you didn't go through the struggles I've been through for years; and now that I am finally on my feet, he wants to come back in and knock me down."

I went on to say, "Sissy, you do not understand because you do not have children. I worked hard every day to hold on to what little I had. I learned to make something out of nothing after he left. I am a tired soul, taking the children to school, daycare, going to school myself, working, running all over the place just to keep my life stable."

I started to cry and said, "I am so tired of people making excuses for these sorry-ass men. They are the ones who decide to leave when things get hard. They are the ones who abandon and neglect to take care of their children. The mother is left to pick up the scattered pieces. The mother has to make up numerous lies to tell her children so they will not be heartbroken because their father isn't in their life. How is that fair to the mother and children? After all the hell I've been through alone with my children, you're telling me it is okay for him to come to see the kids for a couple of hours to clear his conscience and then leave? After he leaves, I'll be left to do everything on my own again; without any help from him. Why do people always have mercy on the fathers of the fatherless children, but turn a blind eye on the mother and never appreciate what a mother does?"

She agreed, and said, "Sis, you are right. I do not have children, but keeping the children away isn't going to solve anything."

I interrupted her and said, "Sis, I am not keeping the children away from him. He was the one that made that choice. All I'm saying is, it isn't fair that he wants to come and "visit" for a couple of hours just to see how much they've grown. Bring a couple of t-shirts, undies, socks, and think he's "father of the year." If I'd waited two years for him to bring the kids t-shirts, they would have been naked. Sad to say, they would have been dead a long time ago, because he sure didn't help financially with food, water, etc. I survived on my own. He didn't want to come back and save the house. He was fine knowing we were going to be homeless on the streets."

Sissy calmly said, "Sis, I understand exactly where you are coming from.

However, the issue you have is with you and him; and the children shouldn't be punished for what he did. Yes, he left the kids. It was wrong, so wrong what he did, but Sis, the children shouldn't be in the middle of the mess that was created."

I told Sissy I respect her for not taking what I said personally. I respect her even more for being brutally honest. I went on to say that sometimes when a person isn't in the situation, they can see better from the outside. Although we had a disagreement, we were woman enough to listen and value each other's opinion. That made our sisterhood stronger. My sissy resides up north and we text and talk every day as if we lived next door to each other.

I love to skate. I've been skating since I was five years old, or maybe younger. My mom and dad are skaters too. They used to take us to the skating rink every Saturday. I guess it runs in the family because my children are skaters as well. With that being said, I met my sister Tenisha at the skating rink. We met through our children. Since day one, we had a good relationship. She has sickle cell anemia and she has her moments where she has a crisis from time to time. I always visited her and we would have a good time bonding in a hospital room. As time went by, we became sisters. When she needed, me, I was always there, and when I needed her, she was there for me too.

One day, when I needed her the most, I felt like she was ignoring me because I had just talked to her a couple of hours before I had a situation occur. She didn't respond to my text messages or calls. I figured out my situation. However, I was upset with her, but I kept it moving.

The next day, she called, but I didn't pick up. She didn't leave a message so I didn't call back. A month went by and I missed my sister. I missed her laugh (which is hilarious), I missed her presence. I decided to call her; she answered. We talked about our faults and moved past the misunderstanding.

As a woman, a true loyal friendship is important. Truth be told, it takes patience and a lot of work. You will have some friendships that will be underestimated and tested. Most definitely, there will some friendships that will come and go. However, there will be friendships and sisterhoods that will last a lifetime. A true sister will walk through the fire with you; and after she walks through the fire, she will stand against the rough currents with you. Nobody is perfect. True sisterhood is a gift that absolutely holds your love together.

In a marriage, a woman has to be the backbone, the compromiser; yet half the time she feels powerless. Marriage isn't easy. There are a lot of pitfalls, steep uphill battles, obstacles, compromises, and sacrifices. As the saying goes, the man is the head of the household, but truth be told, I am still trying to understand how that is so. There are some good men out there who successfully honor their role as a husband and a father to their children. However, there are so many single mothers in the world today who are the heads of households, being both the mother and the father.

As a single mother, I feel like I carry the weight of the ocean on my shoulders trying to keep my head above water to keep from drowning. I try to stand firm as I dig my toes in the sand, but the troubling waves tend to wash the sand away from under my feet. I lose my balance, but I have to make the best of what I am given; take a leap of faith and start swimming.

At times, my children do not understand the pressure. Yet, it goes unnoticed, as if I am "supposed" to supply their "wants." I love my children, but most of the time I feel like they do not understand the load I carry on a daily basis.

Children fail to realize that a mother doesn't have to provide their "wants." Her bags are heavy because they are filled by everyone's "wants." There isn't one "want" in the bags a mother is carrying that belongs to her. She looks past her self-fulfillment. She feels as though her wants and needs are not important; therefore, they are never on the list.

Children cannot see past their selfish ways. By law, a parent is supposed to provide shelter, food, clothing, make sure their children attend schools and have their annual health checkups. A mother isn't required to put her children in extracurricular activities; that is a choice.

Friends come and go; a marriage may last or fail, but once you're a mother there is no such thing as divorcing your children. Being a mother is the hardest job ever; it is "till death do you part." As a mother, you try your best to make sure your children do not make the same mistakes that you did.

Most definitely, you want your children to have more than you had; a better life, education, better opportunities, and more. You want to give your children the love you always wanted or advice you wish you would have gotten. However, over and over again, you are underestimated and criticized. Nothing is ever good enough.

I shifted gears on my children. My kindness was taken for weakness; I felt as though from time to time they would double-team me. At the beginning of the day, it was I, me, Momma, who was providing their needs and wants.

My oldest is twenty years old and legally grown; therefore, he can provide for his own wants and needs. However, I was helping him from time to time, but he never appreciated how I always went out of my way and gave him advice for his own good. Like any young adult who thinks he is grown, he would do the opposite of the advice that was given. With that being said, I had to fall back and let him make his own mistakes in the hope that he would learn from them.

My daughter is seventeen years old; she could work part-time to get her nails, toes, and hair done. She could also purchase accessories and clothes of her liking. Interestingly, I advised her about a couple of places where she could apply for work. She didn't even lift a finger to write her name on an application. Little does she know that I am not going to provide for her "wants"—especially since my kindness is taken for granted.

Both of my oldest children will see that money doesn't grow on trees. Once they start taking responsibility for their "wants" I am more than sure they are going to have a change of heart.

Being a mother isn't an easy task. It has its ups and downs, joy and difficult moments. I wish more children could see that a mother's love should never be undervalued. A mother's love is priceless and unconditional without asking for anything in return except for appreciation, respect, gratitude, and for them to do well in school.

I believe that when children are old enough and can legally work, they need to find a job. Therefore, they will value each penny they earn on their paycheck. It's funny how my children received money from their grandparents and never wanted to spend it, but freely want to spend mine.

There have been a couple of times when we would go out to eat and I would tell them they could all pay for their own meal. I was never concerned as they watched me eat because they didn't want to spend their money. You better believe I let them watch me eat! How ironically, all of a sudden, they would say, "We will find something at home to eat." If I was paying for their meal, they would have ordered exactly what they wanted – with a drink.

If we as mothers can spend our hard-earned money, well, I'll be damned, they can spend their money as well.

I was hip to the "game" and to be honest, the word "No" was like music to my ears.

My oldest son comes to me endlessly asking for money. I tell him he can't be grown when he wants to be a grown man, and a child when he wants to be a little boy. I ended the conversation gently and told him to figure it out.

My daughter wanted money to hang out with her friends. I looked at her and said, "Really? Well, you are seventeen years old; you can work to make money for what you want to do."

I stopped giving out money. I stopped caring for their wants because their wants aren't needs. When they needed a ride somewhere, I told them that if I was Uber, Lyft, or a friend, you would have paid for their time, gas and services. I said, "If you do not have gas money, walk or find another way."

I used to ask my children what they wanted for breakfast, lunch, dinner, or from the grocery store. I stopped asking. I bought what I was going to cook. If they wanted to eat, fine; if not, they could starve. They failed to realize the smallest things—such as asking *what do you want* is a privilege.

I wasn't going to punish my eleven-year-old—I was going to be fair and let him make his own mistakes. From the looks of it, he was quickly learning what *not* to do from his siblings.

Legally, I wasn't responsible for my oldest. As for my daughter, I did what was demanded from me legally. Other than that, I wasn't responsible for paying her phone bill, giving her extra money to hang with her friends, taking her out to eat, buying brand-name clothes, or buying her food of choice.

I took a stand because I was tired of my unconditional love, kind and generous ways being taken for granted. They underestimated me as their mother as if I *had* to do the things I did. No, ma'am, it was a choice.

Being a daughter, granddaughter, and sister isn't easy—some family members rejoice when you're struggling. Sad but true, some family members do not ask if you need a helping hand. They fold their arms as they stand on the sidelines, happily watching you sink. What makes matters worse, they prefer a front-row seat. They want to enjoy seeing how deep you are going to sink. They watch with smirks on their faces, filled with envy and happiness, while at the same time they feel completed instead of remorseful.

I always lend a helping hand, but sadly, the cards that I was dealt were never in my favor. When I visit a particular family member, I cannot ever go to her house empty-handed. I always had to have something in my hand. If not, I would be criticized for something or called the prodigal daughter.

What I never understood was how some people are good at quoting scriptures, but never follow through it entirely. When the prodigal son came back home; he was welcomed with opened arms and a feast. I always wondered, *where was my hug*? I received a hug if I brought food or something worthwhile. I never received a feast. However, I was the one who was bringing the feast. Now how does that work? There were times I didn't visit because I didn't have any spare money in my budget. If I were to visit empty-handed, I would be criticized for showing up with nothing, as opposed to simply showing up out of love. With that being said, my best bet was to not to show up at all. Either way, it was a bad call, and I was blamed for something.

There are many grandmothers, mothers, and siblings who put pressure on their "favorite" person (who most of the time is a female). They underestimate this person and do not appreciate anything they do. Everything their "fav" person attempts to do or say is taken for granted, out of context, or something is always wrong. That plays on a person's mind and lasts for years, if not forever.

Yet, the "fav" person tries to please everyone. The people on the sidelines decided to sail to shore after they got everything they wanted. They didn't even invite their "fav" person to come aboard. Sad to say, sooner than later their boat is going to be too heavy to sail because it's filled to its capacity with their silent, hateful, and distasteful ways.

While they're watching and waiting for your little boat to tip over, their boat is in the process of sinking. While you were going through the storm, you prepared and gathered all the right tools to survive the next storm that was to come; and arrived safely to shore. It would be so much easier if families could come together and share the tools, as opposed to taking pleasure in waiting for the other person to fail.

I wonder why a woman has to work one hundred times harder than her male counterparts. Every time I look around, I see that a woman has to prove to people that she is worthy of the same respect and appreciation that others receive. Why is it that a woman has to compromise her self-worth to please other people and make them happy? Is that fair?

One of my students wasn't happy with her grade. However, that was the grade she was given. During the semester, she was lazy and didn't take the course seriously. In all honesty, she earned a zero, but I gave her a grade of fifty instead.

She would write anything down on her exams; which she failed most of the time. Curves here and there helped her out. Overall, she got a "C" in the class (which she didn't earn). After I submitted the grades, she complained to my supervisors about her final grade. I put up a fight on why I shouldn't change her grade. Long story short, I had to change her grade from a "C" to a "B." I was livid.

One of my counterparts was going through the same situation. However, he didn't have to fight as hard as I did. He said he wasn't changing the student's grade and he went on with his day. I asked him, "What was the outcome?" He said he refused to change the grade and they let him be. It wasn't that easy for me. I put up a fight and had reasons for why I shouldn't change her grade, but the proof I had wasn't good enough. I wondered, *were they trying to prove a point because I am a female.*

As I was walking to my car, the student walked up to me, smiling from ear to ear, and said, "Ms. Jackson, I told you, you were going to change my grade."

I replied, "You're correct. Your grade was changed, but when all is said and done, you cheated yourself. You didn't earn a "B." In reality, you didn't earn a "C"—you really deserved an "F."

She looked at me, smirked and said, "It doesn't matter what I was supposed to have gotten, the point is I got a "B."

Before I walked away, I smiled at her and said, "Yes, you sure did; and I hope you are happy with the grade you were given."

As the higher authority had proved their point, and the student thought she had won the race, I made it my mission to teach the classes that I knew she needed in the upcoming semester. I made sure I would be the only professor teaching the classes, and that each class was a prerequisite course.

The student thought she had power and had gotten one over on me. She learned that cheaters never win. I also learned that I cannot always help everyone out, because my kindness was easily underestimated and taken for weakness. From that point on I gave each student the grade they earned.

I am pleased to say, I was tickled and filled with so much joy when she walked through the doors of three classes she had with me back-to-back. Instead of the smirk I remembered on her face last time, she was looking like, "*what the hell?*" She knew she couldn't drop the classes because they were required courses. Truly, I did not show her any mercy. I smiled every day as I walked into class. Each grade she got, she earned. I'm sure the next time she will choose her battles wisely.

A woman's strength and character shouldn't ever be underestimated, although time and time again women are taken for granted. A woman has a choice; just like anyone else on this earth—she doesn't have to give her all for her family, friends, or co-workers.

Women are human, just like everyone else. However, a woman is treated as though she's not. It is beyond ridiculous that a woman always has to justify her actions in lengthy detail in every situation and the person she encounters.

A woman's strength is unstoppable as she takes on the loads she is given in life. We, as women, shouldn't ever underestimate our ability. We are warriors, and if it wasn't for our great strength of perseverance, what would the world be like today?

We have to learn how to put ourselves first. We have to stop cheating ourselves by putting other people's needs first, and our needs and wants last.

When I let go of everyone's problems and focused on me, I gained a lot of knowledge about myself I didn't know. I finally realized the definition of peace, joy, love, and happiness. When I started to give more to myself, I learned to love myself wholeheartedly.

Most importantly, I learned that nobody would love me more than I love myself. I am the only person who will love hard on me. Therefore, I learned how to live in a self-fulfilling mode, and I wouldn't have it any other way!

AFFIRMATION

"Ladies, it's harvest time!!! Take care of your crops, water them and weed them out."

Sacrifices and Resentments

We live in a cruel world. People are dreadfully cold. I have never seen so many dishonest, selfish and greedy people. They are willing to use others until they get exactly what they want. What makes matters even worse, after they get what they want, they come back and ask for more. Sadly, people do not have any empathy for others. They are like leeches and will suck the blood out of you until you have nothing left.

When you can't provide for them anymore, their true character comes out. They treat you like pure shit. To make matters worse, they talk trash behind your back, as if what you've done for them was useless. Once you don't have anything to give they will label you as the weak link. That's how some people are—they will use you up and break you down until you have nothing left to give them or yourself. People who do not have anything to lose will make sure you lose everything you've worked so hard for.

A woman sacrifices more than she is given, and nobody is willing to take any of the pain that they have caused. Yet she is running at full speed without a break, and her world is crumbling from carrying everyone else's problems. Where are the extended hands? They are nowhere to be found.

A woman lives with resentment. Resentment hurts, and it is a throbbing pain that leaves deep scars. Although some of the scars heal, the resentment lingers on. When she kneels to pray, she feels as if her prayers fall on deaf ears; the burdens are intolerable.

Sacrifices and resentments leave a woman standing on the edge, but she doesn't have the nerve to look down or jump. As a woman struggles through the day she tried to soothe the hurt, but every time she turns around it spreads like wildfire. She is left alone in the middle of a crisis. As women, we ask ourselves over and over again, *how long do I have to wait? When will the torture end?*

Look deep within your soul and ask yourself—no matter who it concerns—is it worth it?

Is it worth losing your outer and inner peace?

Is it worth your happiness?

Is it worth your sanity?

If they are causing you stress; let them go and cut the cord.

The question that needs to be asked is—who do you love more? Yourself, or making other people happy?

If I knew then what I know now—I would have chosen me. I would have loved me more. I would have put a smile on my face. I would have made sure I laughed at least three times a day or more; the more the better. I would have fallen in love with the peace that was surrounding me. Self-fulfillment is what I would have given more of to myself.

Sadly, a lot of things took a turn for the worse in my life, but they taught me a lesson. They helped me to become the person I am today. In my late thirties, I am learning so much about myself, and still learning. I am so in love with myself more than I've ever been! I feel free and at peace. Life is good! It is getting better and better every day!

There are stages in life that you must go through to find out the true value of your worth. I learned that nobody knows your worth but you. Nobody will value you, more than yourself. People will treat you according to how much you can take.

Do you know how much you can take? Do you know your limits?

I had to go through hell and beyond to answer both questions. When I look back, I ask myself, *who's to blame?*

When I was in my late teenage years and in my early twenties, I used to take my grandmother to church every Wednesday and Sunday, to revivals, and whenever they had something special going on. I was young, vibrant and pretending to be happy, but I was miserable because I was treated so unfairly. It was as though I was "trained" to think and dress a certain way. I always wore the same long black skirt that went past my ankles, and the same black clogs.

If I wore anything else my grandmother would consider me as dressing 'naked.' I wasn't the type of person to dress inappropriately because I respect myself and how I carry myself. As I look back, I realize I was controlled by her. My grandmother had the power to make me feel happy—and to feel like shit if she wanted to.

At that time, I felt like I was a dog on a leash. When my grandmother called me, I would stop what I was doing and be at her beck and call. However, nothing was ever good enough. I felt like my soul was ripped from my core. I felt I was a dead woman walking.

What made matters worse, my sisters and I used to always be there for my grandmother, but we were treated so badly. We were told we were only good for making babies. She always talked badly about us—yet she called on my sisters and me to do this and that all the time.

I guess my grandmother felt like she had the right to treat us the way she did because we lived next door to her for half of our lives. We were like her children that she didn't give birth to. To this day, she says, "You are my baby; you are my child. I raised you as my own. Your mother birthed you into this world, but you are my baby."

I would say, "Yes, Grandmother, I am your baby."

What's so sad, the cycle never ended; it continued. When I was in high school, my oldest sister used to buy my grandmother groceries every month. However, after she went out of her way to do that, my grandmother would talk down to her to the point that it broke her spirit for years. My grandmother always made my sister cry by telling her what she wasn't going to be, or what she couldn't do, or what she was *only* going to do. Yet my sister continued to supply my grandmother with groceries.

I remember asking my sister, "Why do you let Grandma treat you like that?" My sister never had an answer. I believe it was the same reason why I did; mainly because I felt like I owed her my life. When I was younger, my grandmother used to say, "I raised you, and don't you ever forget it."

As I got older, I never forgot it. It was in my head; it controlled my mind. I guess it was programmed in my sister's mind as well. One day, out of the blue, my sister said she'd had enough, and she was tired of crying and tired of trying. She finally broke away from the mistreatment.

Years later.

I then begin to supply my grandmother with groceries. Why in the hell did I do that? I guess I thought my grandmother had changed, but she hadn't. I felt like I was making my grandmother happy. Yet the more I thought I was making her happy, the unhappier I was.

My grandmother would say, "Child, what are you doing? You have those kids to provide for. You do not have to do all of this for me."

There were several times I went to go visit my grandmother empty-handed. I didn't have any food visible. It was only my children and me walking up the steps. As we walked into her house, she was looking around to see if I'd brought something.

Why did I go empty-handed?

I didn't hear the end of it. I was scolded left and right.

The next time I visited, I brought groceries; and I felt loved.

It is very true that actions speak louder than words. I was accepted and loved for what I could give; not who I was as a person.

Needless to say, years went by and nothing changed. The more I tried, the more I was mentally broken down, piece by piece. Nobody knew, but I fell into a deep state of depression. I was very good at hiding it with a smile, but inside, I was torn. I felt like I didn't have any fight left.

Until one day, when I was at church, an older lady on the Mother's Board said, "Mother, your granddaughter is always right by your side. You are so blessed."

My grandmother said, "All of my grandchildren are worthless." She began to talk so badly about me in front of people. I felt humiliated and embarrassed.

I quietly took her home, and after that, I didn't talk to her for a year or so. During that year, I was at peace. I found a little bit of myself. I laughed more. I smiled more, and I kept myself busy in a positive, productive way.

I never understood how someone can say they love a person yet, break them down to the core.

When I was younger, I always told myself; if I have children, I am going to love them for who they are, not for what they can give.

After a year or so passed, I visited my grandmother. She looked at me for a while with a straight face and said, "Well, well, well, the prodigal daughter has come home."

Wow, that was a distasteful, cutthroat, and cold welcome.

(If you're wondering, yes, most definitely, I had something in my hand!)

I felt like I gave my grandmother back her power over me again because I felt so guilty. I felt like I'd done something horribly wrong.

(Before I walked into her house, I sat in the car and asked myself, *are you sure you want to go through with this again*? If I had to ask myself that, what was the point of facing the storm? I knew what I was going up against. Yet, I suited up and prepared for what was to come.)

As my slight smile turned down, she went on to say, "You left me. You forgot all about me."

All I heard was 'me.' Me. Me. Me. Me.

In my mind, I was thinking, *what about me*? I sat there in a daze, thinking and wondering, *why did I come here*?

I blocked her out as she talked because I didn't want to hear or receive her negative energy. I found myself saying, "Yes, ma'am" to everything she said.

After a while, I gave my grandmother a hug and said, "I love you."

As I walked to the door, she said, "You said you love me, but your actions speak louder than your words."

I didn't say anything. As I walked down the steps, I hung my head down in distress. I asked myself, *damn, when will enough be enough? Why is this lady never happy? Goodness, what will it take?*

A couple of weeks passed. My grandmother called. I didn't answer. I was like hell no, not today. I did not feel like being scolded, because I was having a great day.

Days passed and she called every single day. Fussing on my voice mail.

My children and I went to the movies and had a wonderfully happy day!

My grandmother called my phone all day long. After we left the movies, I paid her a visit.

I sat in the car for a while. As I got out of the car, I said to myself, *get it together, do not let her get in your head. Take the hits but make sure they miss your mind.*

I slowly walked up the steps and knocked on the door.

My uncle answered and said, "Oh, it's only Lena and Sarah. I thought you were Patrick." (Patrick is my second cousin who resides in Stone Mountain, not far from Atlanta at all. They were acting like he was flying from another state or out the country).

I was saying to myself, *damn—only Lena and Sarah. Shit, you all been calling my phone all day! I came out of my way to hear, "Oh, it's only Lena and Sarah."* I closed my eyes and shook my head.

I walked into the dining room. They had snacks prepared. I said, "It looks yummy."

My uncle said, "It's for Patrick."

I didn't touch anything. I walked into the living room and sat down on the couch.

My grandmother walked into the living room and said, "Oh, Lena, I didn't know you were coming. I thought you were Patrick."

I smiled.

She went on to say, "Where have you been? Running the streets? I've been calling you and calling you."

I said, "Grandma, I've been here."

She said, "You haven't been "here." I know that for sure."

The doorbell rang. It was my cousin.

My grandmother said, "Well, Lena, you can go home now, because I am going to talk to Patrick."

I didn't even warm up the seat for two minutes. I looked at my daughter and said to myself, *Damn. Really? Okay.*

As Patrick walked through the door we spoke and gave each other a hug. He asked me some questions and it turned into a short conversation.

My grandmother said firmly, "Lena, didn't I tell you, you need to go home now?" She frowned and pointed her finger at the door and said, "Now, go on home now!"

As I stepped one foot out the door my grandmother stood up and walked to the door. As she was walking, she was talking, and shaking her finger at me, saying, "Don't forget to bring me my meat." (she's a vegan, but she called her vegan bacon 'meat').

I couldn't believe this shit. First, she blew up my phone, then I went out of my way to go over there to make sure everything was okay. What made matters worse—I was treated like pure shit after I'd been having a fantastic day! Just a second ago she was scolding me as she literally kicked me out of the house, and now she was asking me for her vegan bacon.

I couldn't believe it! In a way, yes, I did. That is how they treated my siblings and me.

I said, "Of course, Grandma. I will bring you your meat."

When I got in the car, my daughter said, "Momma, I cannot believe what just happened. Why does big momma always treat you so badly? Then she asked you for some food after she kicked us out."

I looked at my daughter, smiled, and said, "We are going to the store to get her what she wants and then, I'm done."

I was so hurt because I thought maybe she would have learned her lesson from previous times. However, nothing had changed. I told my daughter, "Regardless of what I do, it will never be enough." I took it as a granddaughter's love would be never good enough or accepted.

I went to the grocery store and got all the vegan bacon that was on the shelf. I went back to my grandmother's house. I asked my daughter if she could take the food up there.

I rolled down the window.

My uncle came to the door. I heard him say, "What are you all doing back here?"

Sarah gave him the bag. He looked in the bag and his whole attitude changed. He smiled and said, "Oh, oh, okay. Thanks."

That was the last time I saw my grandmother for a year or so.

I was filled with resentment because of the sacrifices I'd made all my life.

I was hurt, disappointed and filled with so much anger. When she or my uncle called, I never answered. It got to the point they stopped calling altogether. I told myself I wasn't going to ever go down that road again.

I love myself too much to be treated that way. I deserved better. Hell, as much as I did, I should have been appreciated, not taken for granted and insulted. As I tried to mend the broken pieces, I tore down the remains and built a new foundation of strength in my mind, and in my physical appearance. I had to look deep within because I was broken and shattered for decades. Countless times I had patched up the hurt and pain, but I couldn't patch it up anymore; it was time for me to rebuild, restore a new me, and renew my soul and spirit.

As I worked on myself and prayed for us both, I wondered, *why does my grandmother hurt me so badly inside*? I remembered a conversation we'd had when I was eighteen years old. It was a beautiful spring day. My grandmother looked out the window and said, "Look at the pink roses." I stood beside her and said, "They are so beautiful! The center of the flower is yellow with a little touch of blue."

My grandmother then said, "We all have beauty deep inside that is never seen."

She walked over and sat down on the couch. The sun was shining brightly. She asked me to close the curtains. As I closed the curtains, she closed her eyes. I watched her and wondered what she was thinking.

She said, "Lena, as a young girl I always wanted to sing. I used to sing on my daddy's land as I milked the cows, gathered the eggs, and as my momma braided my hair. I used to skip and sing as I went to school and as I laid out in the field. I used to sing as loud as I could. I wanted to go on the road singing, but my daddy wouldn't approve. I loved singing and I still love it until this day."

As she was talking, I was smiling, yearning to hear more.

She opened her eyes and said, "Lena, I was a daddy's girl. I loved my daddy. I did everything I could do to make him proud of me. You know, I wasn't going to marry your granddaddy, because my daddy didn't approve. I begged Daddy to give me away, but he turned his back and said, "No, Lizzie!"

He was so disappointed in me. I got married on my daddy's porch, but he didn't give me away. I was so hurt and disappointed. After I got married, I left; and my daddy didn't talk to me as often because he was disappointed in me."

As I looked back at our conversation, I realized that my grandmother gave up so much of herself to make her daddy happy. She didn't live the life she wanted. She lived her life through her dreams and imagination, which kept her from living and being free. My grandmother wanted more in life, but she settled all her life to make her daddy happy; which wasn't enough. At age fifteen she was married and became my granddaddy's wife; and eventually, she became the mother of eight children; not to mention the miscarriages she had.

Sometimes I wonder, *does my grandmother treat her children and some of her grandchildren the way she does because of her past?* My grandmother was very strict when my mother was a child and teenager. When my mother was a young lady she wanted to be a model, but my grandmother didn't allow her to do it. I would have thought my grandmother would have broken the cycle and let my mother live her dream since my grandmother's father stopped my grandmother from living hers.

When my siblings and I were younger, my grandmother was very strict. I believe that's all she knew, and that was her way of showing her love because that was what she was given.

My grandmother felt as though women shouldn't go to school. She was a firm believer that it was okay for a man to attend school, but not a woman. Again, my grandmother raised her children according to what she was taught. There were times when my grandmother told my siblings and me when we were little girls that we could do anything we put our minds to. I believe she told us that because we were innocent at the time.

As we got older and started to accomplished things in life, I believe my grandmother was resentful. She then told us that women shouldn't do certain things a man does. She didn't believe a woman should be a preacher, lead the country or become mayor, etc. I believe my grandmother had the mentality that a woman should know her place in this world. She failed to realize that times had changed.

When my oldest sister became pregnant, my grandmother told my sister she needed to get married. My daddy was against it. My grandmother rode my sister's mind until she went to the courthouse and got married without anyone knowing. My daddy was beyond pissed off. When my other sister got pregnant, my grandmother told her she should get married. My daddy said, "You got one of my girls to make a huge mistake. I am not going to let you brainwash my other girls to throw their lives away."

When I was in college, my grandmother told me that I wasn't going to graduate because at the time I was divorced and had three little kids. I managed to graduate from undergraduate school with the help and support from my closest friends. When my grandmother found out I was in graduate school getting my Masters, she told me that was impossible. When I graduated, she told me she was going to my graduation to see for her own two eyes that I was walking across the stage to receive my Master's degree.

I feel that when family and friends attend a graduation, it's supposed to be because they are happy and proud of your accomplishments, hard work and dedication. Not to see if it's for real. Well, one thing was for sure—her eyes weren't playing tricks on her. I earned my degree and walked across the stage with pride and honor!

As I healed from the anger, I was filled with resentment. I learned a person can forgive, but resentment lingers on, filling the heart with so much pain. Resentment leaves your spirit numb while the scars slowly heal and you deal with the pain.

I have noticed that as you try to heal, people do not respect your request for peace. They prick you like the quills of a porcupine. If they see you happy, they try to disturb your aura. When they see that you've moved on in life, you'd better watch out because they will find a way to drop a manipulative bomb on you somehow.

When I was working on rebuilding myself spiritually, physically, and emotionally, my oldest sister kept calling me, saying, "Grandma wants to hear from you. You should call her."

My mother would send me a text, pulling the "sick" card, saying, "Grandma isn't feeling well. You should visit her because she really wants to see you." I didn't fall for that. The best thing I could do at that time was pray for her.

The cycle continued and I thought, "*Goodness gracious, what about me? Does anyone care about how I feel?*"

A couple of months passed and my sister came by to visit me with her grandson. She said, "I just came from Grandma's house."

I replied, "That's awesome!"

She said, "Well, Grandma asked about you, and she wants to see you. Every time I talk to her, she asks about you."

I rolled my eyes, smiled and said, "I'm more than sure she does." I then asked her what she took to Grandma's house because I knew she didn't go empty-handed.

She laughed and said, "I brought a case of water."

I laughed. She then said, "Okay, Lena, you are going to do what you want to do. Talking to you is like beating a dead horse."

I looked her straight in the eyes and said, "Well, why are you talking to me about it? I am finally at peace. I am loving life and I want to continue to love life. I do not want to be torn down anymore. That's was the old me. I have experienced a rebirth and I am new, shining and improved. I will go up there to see her when I am good and ready. Until then, I have to love and work on myself."

I think when people know you are well within yourself, they do not like it because they haven't gotten to that point in their life. I was strong-willed and I was determined that when I had healed from the resentment, I would come around; other than that, I was happy in my cocoon.

When you are healing yourself, you have to make up your mind that there isn't room for compromise. You cannot compromise your self-worth, your peace, your joy, your happiness, for anyone. There is no such thing as half-assed self-healing. Either you are going to give yourself your full and undivided attention or you going to let people destroy your peace and/or life.

Nowadays, people's back-biting runs deep; now children are quick to throw their parents under the bus. Now, people are so cold-hearted and they will do just about anything to get themselves out of the mess they created for themselves; even if it consists of hurting their mother. A mother goes through so much; yet nothing is ever, ever good enough, even though she gives her all.

I wish that a mother could become invisible and see how her children would live life without her help. I wonder how in the world they would survive.

I love my children. I believe I did a good job raising them, but I've learned that when they realize they have minds of their own, they do not make wise decisions. They are not perfect. The issue is, will they take with them what they've learned or will they forget it all?

Well, my oldest son lives in his own world. He thinks he can turn on the switch and snap his fingers and everything will work out in his favor. If it doesn't, he comes out of the world he made and blames everyone for his mistakes. He never looks at himself to see where he went wrong. However, when things go his way he has the mindset that he did it all on his own. Um, really?

He has the tendency to look out for himself, and himself only. His selfishness is dangerous. He comes up with ideas, which is great, but he never thinks before he executes the plan. He just goes along without thinking about the "what if's" and when it doesn't work out as he planned, he has an excuse for everything.

During prom season my son didn't want to attend prom. I asked him if he was sure. He said yes. At that time, he was in his senior year. I told him he should attend prom. He made the final decision and said he didn't want to go.

Two days before the prom, he decided he *did* want to go to the prom. I was excited! I couldn't believe he was in the 12th grade going to the prom. Time goes by so fast.

However, this was short notice.

We went to Men's Warehouse and fitted him for a tux in maroon and gray. He was so handsome. I was a proud mother; as I should have been. I wanted to take tons of pictures here and there. I asked him to turn around so I could get a good picture. He was like, "Mom, you will get more pictures during prom."

I only took four pictures at the Men's Warehouse.

Four.

I was pissed! I wanted to say, "Take that shit off!" I could have kept my money, not to mention, I paid for overnight shipping since prom was in two days. He should have been more than happy to let me take all the pictures my heart desired.

Not knowing that the worst was yet to come, on the day of the prom, I wanted to help him get ready. Instead, the first thing that came out of his mouth was, "Momma, when you meet my prom date and her parents, do not embarrass me."

Basically, he was telling me to be on my best behavior. Where the hell did that come from? I was fed up and I told him, "If you think I'm going to act like a fool, then why bother asking me to show up?" I was highly disappointed because I had never embarrassed my son. I was there to get him out of all of his many troubles in high school. I was a concerned parent and always gave my best effort. I always fought for him. For him to say, "Momma, don't embarrass me." I felt like he didn't want me there. We got into a huge argument, then he went to my neighbor's house and they helped him get ready.

I didn't see him off to the prom. My neighbors took him, and one of his friends drove him to his prom date's house.

After carrying my son, giving birth to him and giving him all the love I had, the hard work and struggles I'd been through with him, I couldn't enjoy the prom. Something I'd been waiting for since he was born. That shit cut deep; deep to the core.

I tried to love my son the best I could. I gave him all I could, and I helped him to the best of my abilities. However, what I did wasn't enough.

I noticed that my son wanted me there for the bad times and to help get him out of the messes he created for himself, but he never wanted me there to celebrate the good times.

During prom night, I cried from hurt and pain; and I asked myself, *what have I done to deserve such treatment?* I wasn't the perfect mother, who is? I began to think about all of the sacrifices I'd made and how I was now filled with so much resentment.

I cried and cried because when a mother knows she has done all she can do and worked her ass off for her children, when no appreciation is given, it hurts.

I felt empty.

His friend sent me a picture of the young lady and my son; she was beautiful and he was so handsome. However, seeing them with the naked eye would have meant the world to me. However, I didn't want to "embarrass" him." Whatever that meant.

Some of my friends said I should have gone anyway. After all the messes my son had presented to me, I was tired of him being disrespectful. I was tired of hiding my feelings. I was tired of ignoring my pain. If I had gone, I would have had to put on a fake smile and act as if everything was okay. I was tired of the fake smiles. My son meant what he said, and I took it at face value.

My son had put a hurting on me so badly.

My oldest sister got her son and daughter a senior jacket; she ordered them from their school. Of course, it cost a pretty penny to purchase them. My sister worked hard and made payments on their jackets because she knew how badly her children wanted them. They appreciated their letterman jackets and wore them all the time!

On the other hand, I worked hard too. Extra hard, because my son's school wasn't ordering jackets for the athletes or seniors. I went online and handpicked his jacket; it was hard to find a royal blue and gray letterman jacket. However, I found the right jacket in his school colors, real leather sleeves, and heavy wool. It was nice!!

Once I found the jacket, I had to pick out the right letters and find the perfect mascot, which was difficult! However, I had the jacket custom-made and ordered it. I searched high and low for the bulldog mascot and for tennis ball patches. Of course, I found and ordered them. The plan was to have them sewn on to the coat.

When my son saw the jacket, he was happy, but he complained about what was wrong with the jacket. He never wore it once.

I overheard his friends say one day, "Man, you have a letterman jacket! I wish I had one!"

Again, giving him something that I thought he was going to be proud to wear was a waste of time, money and energy. Children are so ungrateful.

As I sobbed quietly, I begin to think about the time I took my daughter to CVS for a physical because she wanted to join the cheerleading squad. I gave my son some money and asked him to buy me a Twix. He brought it back with my change, and I said thank you. I asked him to watch my little one as I stayed with Sarah while she was being examined.

Next thing I knew, a man asked if could he speak with me for a moment.

I told him no.

However, he said, "Ma'am, I am an undercover police officer."

He took us to the storage room and told me they have my son (who at the time was fifteen going on sixteen) on camera, eating Reese Pieces, and he told my little one to be on the lookout.

I was like, *"What the hell! You have got to be kidding me!"* I really thought the officer was joking, because who in their right mind would do that?

The officer asked my son why he ate the Reese's Pieces. My son said, "Because my momma doesn't give me any attention."

My daughter and my little one looked at my oldest son with their mouths wide open. My mouth was open too. I experienced a sharp pain in my heart. I was in shock. I couldn't believe what came out of his mouth.

I made sure I was at every tennis practice and game. I was always supportive. I made sure I was there to listen when he needed an ear. One thing's for sure, my actions spoke louder than my words. It was well known that other people saw how much attention, work, and support I put into my children's lives on a daily basis.

The officer said to him, "I refuse to believe that because I watched you all as you walked into the store. Your mother asked you to get her something and she said thank you. After you brought it back, she said thank you again. It isn't common for a mother in this neighborhood to say thank you to her children."

He went on to say, "I see your mother has structure in the household. Again, why did you steal and eat the candy? And why did you ask your little brother to be on the lookout? What kind of example are you setting for him?"

My oldest son said, "I do not know."

The officer said, "Ma'am, do you want me to arrest him?"

I wanted to say, hell yeah, lock his ass up. I was filled with so much anger, hurt and disappointment. My mind was going a million miles per hour. I thought I was going to have a heart attack because I was still in shock from my son's actions and words. I was wondering, *why would he do this and why would he say that? Why?"*

I answered and said, "No, sir. Please let him come home with me."

The officer looked at my son and said, "And you said your mother doesn't love you. At the moment, she is livid. If she didn't love you, she would have had your ass locked up. She loves you so much to the point that she isn't letting her anger control the outcome. Nor did she let her anger and your lies get the best of her. Truthfully, if I was her, I would have locked your ass up to teach you a lesson."

He took a couple of steps, turned around and said, "Young man, normally I wouldn't ask a parent, do you want me to lock your son up? I asked your mother because I noticed your mother has structure and her children are well behaved. If it was any other officer, they would have locked you up without any questions asked."

I didn't want my son to be labeled as a menace to society. I wanted him to have a clean record so he would be able to go to college and have a fruitful life.

I do not know how many times I am willing to let my heart get kicked to the ground. My son took it to another level; this time my heart was stomped into the ground. As if I do not have more than enough people to kick me down! I was shattered inside, and on the outside, I was so fragile. Once again, I took a chance. I took another fall, but I was not broken.

I have come to the conclusion that a mother's love is never good enough.

Every time I turned around, I felt weighed down over something my son did to save his own ass. I have to let my son live and learn, and only time will tell.

As a woman, it's hard to stay grounded when every time you think you are doing something right, someone wants to pull up the roots you took so long to plant. What adds insult to injury is—it isn't your shit.

A woman is always carrying other people's burdens, kicked to the ground, scorned, and damaged to the core. When a woman is going along at a steady pace, someone comes along to knock her off balance. A woman falls more often than she likes to. That's okay, give yourself a shake and dust it off. A woman can be bruised many times, but she is not broken, and she always rises above it.

As a woman, you are always empowering others and helping people out of their situations. The time has come, and the time is now, for you to take charge of your own journey. It doesn't matter how young or how old you are. It is time for you to freefall into giving yourself a chance at love, and the first person you should fall in love with is yourself.

There are too many women who haven't had the chance to fall in love with themselves. Your sacrifices weren't for nothing. Each sacrifice you made was by choice to help others as you put them first. With each sacrifice that you made, you took chances, and the uphill battles of carrying the weight on your shoulders toned your core.

Each sacrifice was a process of change. Your tears changed your perception and they cleansed your soul. Those were survival tears. As you were changing, slowly but surely you were forming a connection as you began to think and analyze—this isn't your life. This isn't you.

Change gives you the courage to look at your past without any regrets. Change says your past made you stronger and wiser and is getting you ready to emerge from hibernation. It is preparing you to never comprise your self-worth and to take everything at face value. Take a breather. Don't underestimate your ability to create your own happiness. Your journey starts when you begin to love (Y.O.U.) Yourself. Over. Unhappiness.

AFFIRMATION

"Don't bury yourself in broken dreams of resentment. Expand your life purpose and reap the benefit of happiness!"

Fallen Warrior

A woman is mistreated and disrespected on so many levels, yet she is the one who makes the curves in the road straight. She is the one who smoothes the bumpy road. When a woman loves; she loves hard, and when she loves hard, she loves deeply from within the core of her soul. Yet, she is never appreciated.

A woman is always being taken advantage of in so many situations. To add insult to injury, people always try to belittle a woman—as if her opinion doesn't matter, people feel that they can manipulate a woman as if she's naïve and clueless. Other people will steal a woman's idea as if they came up with it on their own. It makes my skin crawl when a woman is told to step aside and keep quiet as if her voice doesn't deserve to be heard, and we all know that women don't receive as many opportunities as their male counterparts. However, opportunities are endless, and when a woman is given a chance, she makes it a personal mission to execute by always being the seeker and observer.

Education is very important. The more education a woman has the more she is looked down upon. Nothing comes easy for a woman, and that is why she is tough. She has to earn everything she works hard for—that's fine, and honestly, it isn't an issue. Hard work grooms a woman to be a powerful force.

I received an email for an emergency meeting and wondered what could possibly be wrong. During the meeting, I felt awkward because I was the only female in the room. With great concern, I asked a co-worker of mine. "Why am I the only female in this meeting?"

As he flipped the pen in his hand, he didn't take his eyes off his paper.

He cleared his throat and said, "We do not want to appear as though we are being biased. Therefore, we made the decision to have at least one female in the room for our meeting."

The answer alone was biased—I knew that as men they intended to dominate the meeting and ignore me without allowing me to voice my opinion.

Before the meeting started, they passed around the roster for everyone to sign (stating we attended the meeting). The roster was proof that they had a female in the meeting; therefore, they covered their tracks to avoid discrimination. As the meeting proceeded, questions were being asked. I had an answer for each individual question. I was either overlooked and/or someone would talk over me with an answer that didn't relate to the question. I was frustrated because I was being disrespected in so many ways.

I guess they thought I was going to sit back and let them walk all over me. However, I waited for the right moment to lay down the foundation of my thoughts to solve the problem. The president of the company joined the meeting after two hours because he wanted an update. Sad to say, none of the issues were resolved. However, I wrote down an answer to all of the questions that were asked. I created a "formula" that supported my claim step by step and waited until all of the men had finished their presentations. I stood up and executed my game plan with results that would work. Not only would it work, but it would produce growth in the company; such as taking the company to a higher level of respect and an increase in revenue.

Of course, the president was impressed! I wasn't surprised. He asked the men in the meeting, "Why did it take two hours to come up with this plan (my plan) and why did you all waste another hour of my time with the rubbish you all presented to me? Charlena, had the master plan, and she was finally allowed to present it."

I waited for someone to answer. The room was completely silent. I broke the silence and said, "Well, truth be told, my opinion didn't matter to them. I tried to participate in the meeting, but I was either being disrespected by being talked over, walked over, or not heard. Basically, I was being overlooked because I am a woman." I added, "I was told I am the only woman in the meeting because they didn't want to appear biased."

The president didn't say a word. That really pissed me off. I looked him dead in the eyes and said, "You do not think this is gender discrimination?"

His exact words were, "Charlena, do not be silly now. Don't you think you are taking this out of proportion?" He tried to laugh it off as if I was going to be passive about this serious issue.

He continued and said, "Charlena, I loved your presentation! If you will sign the documents for approval of use, we will let Albert present it to our potential client." He slapped the table with joy and said, "I know we are going to have them in the bag and they are going to proceed with our company for sure!"

As he proceeded to walk out the door, he had a pep in his step, smiling from ear to ear, saying, "We are going to have them eating out of the palms of our hands!"

I sat back in my chair and watched him. I guess he really thought I was going to hand over my hard work willingly and forget about what had just happened—again.

As he reached the door, I stood up and said, "With all due respect, I might add, you all haven't shown or given me any respect. You walked all over everything I just expressed. No, I am not taking it "out of proportion." This is a serious issue, and as a woman, I am being used and treated unfairly."

He tried to cut me off. I interrupted him and said, "Let me finish. I am tired of being cut off. That is a form of disrespect." I continued, "I am not signing over my work. My voice wasn't being heard; nor are you hearing me out now. Do you think I am going to hand over my work for *Albert* to present? Do you seriously think I am going to walk out of this building and not file a gender discrimination report?"

He walked back into the room. Sat in his chair and leaned to the side as if he didn't give a shit, and he said, "Charlena, okay, let's talk."

I told him, "No, it is too late to talk. Women in your company are always being disrespected, but we work our asses off to keep this company afloat, and men like you use our work and ideas as your own. Not anymore!

Today, it stops on my watch!"

He acted like he was concerned and said, "Charlena, we will have a mandatory meeting to address the issue."

I laughed and said, "Now you want to have a mandatory meeting so you can act like you care? Please, this serious matter has been circulating around the company for years by word, emails, meetings, yet nothing has been done, and truth be told, nothing will be done until we, as women, take a stand."

I walked to the door and said, "I've taken enough for way too long. Once the word spreads around the company, and it will in a nanosecond, I wish you the best because your company is going to crumble to the ground without the women's help."

I smiled and said, "A woman's hard work is never good enough. Next time, you will value a woman's hard work and creativity."

I walked out, came right back in and said, "Oh, and Chuck, by the way, I quit!"

I felt good when I walked out the door. I walked with pride and my strides were light but powerful.

I always felt as though I was a fallen warrior at this company because nothing that a woman did was ever good enough for her to present. However, her work was good enough for a man to present and receive all the credit. How sexist, disrespectful and thoughtless!

It is really sad because women are fallen warriors at their jobs since they are always either under pressure, suffer from peer pressure and/or threatened. Most of the time, a woman is silent because she's afraid of losing her job.

I had a friend who was being mistreated at her workplace. She felt as though she had to take what she was given without question. She fell into a deep state of depression because her options for promotion at the company were slim to none. She applied for other positions but she wasn't qualified; therefore, she settled, because she needed her job to provide for her children and herself.

Her job was very stressful and she became a fallen warrior because she was being threatened; if she didn't suit up for the job, she was going to be laid off. She was giving more than her job description outlined, without any increase in pay. What made matters worse, she qualified for a higher position, but it was given to a man. She continued to apply for other jobs, but nothing came through. She worked at her job for a couple of years and worked a part-time job during the midnight hours until she saved enough money to start her own business.

A woman is constantly on a treadmill because she is always judged and treated unfairly. If she gives too much, it is overlooked. If she does the minimum, she will be ridiculed. A woman is never in the clear and her hard work is never good enough. Women are manipulated on a daily basis by someone who feels like they have the right to overpower a woman.

Beneath the surface a woman is not passive; she is amassing her strength. At times she might bend, but she does not break. There are times she will become a fallen warrior, but she knows how to rise from the ashes.

A friend of mine called me on a daily basis, crying about how her co-workers took advantage because she was a female. Her job description was, as they said, a "manly" job. Really? There isn't such a thing as a "manly" job; a woman can do anything a man can do. She was told at her workplace that she should get on a pole to entertain men for an eight-hour shift. There were times when she was slapped on her butt, and she was asked by the men at her job, did she wear a bra or did she want to be "manly?"

She complained to her boss. He responded, "That is what's wrong with women; you're all so sensitive. I do not understand why you can't take a joke. That's why this is a man's job and no women should be allowed."

His response shattered her confidence because she was a fallen warrior who felt like she didn't have a voice. What she complained about wasn't taken seriously and was ignored.

She was the only female on the night shift, and the men put a sign on the unisex restroom door which read, "No Women Allowed." One night, as she used the restroom, one of her co-workers walked in, blocked her in the stall and touched her inappropriately. As she ran out of the restroom, everyone was laughing. She was a fallen warrior who felt defeated, dirty, nasty and disrespected on so many levels.

Needless to say, she left and didn't complete her shift.

The next day, she received a call that she was fired for "walking out on the job." She tried explaining to her boss what had happened but he didn't want to hear it.

She gathered her proof and followed the chain of command. It was a tough fight for almost a year. She kept pushing for her voice to be heard. It was hard to contact the right person in Corporate, however, when she finally got someone to listen, an investigation was put into action.

I am proud to say, her former boss and all of the men on the night shift were fired, and she pressed charges for sexual assault, discrimination, and harassment.

Women have been disrespected in the workplace on so many levels over the years, and it goes unnoticed and ignored.

Not anymore!

Today, we take a stand!

There are many movements such as Me Too and Time's Up that are representing and helping the fallen warriors to stand up for justice; to stand up to be treated equally; to stand up and say *"NO, NOT TODAY; NOT ANYMORE!"*

As a fallen warrior, you feel like nothing has been going your way lately, and that you do not have any fight left. Do not dwell on the past or what is thrown at you; instead, use it as fuel to be a powerful fighter! As you become a powerful fighter, learn how to balance and focus on your inner peace. Keep a steady, positive mind and remind yourself that nobody has the power or authority to bring you down.

When someone hurts your pride, do not allow them to force you to run away or lose hope. They want you to struggle, they want you to feel like you are suffocating, and they want you to feel like you cannot go on. Let go of wasted negative energy and fear —you are only human and you cannot please everyone at the same time. Remember, nobody can take your inner peace unless you allow them to.

It is okay to cry survival tears. In difficult times, it is okay to ask questions. It is hard to let go and have faith; therefore, you are always asking, Why me? What did I do wrong? Should I have given more of this or that? Or, what if?

Stop.

Pause.

If you start to overthink, you start thinking wrong. Calm your mind and know, Fallen Warrior, this is not your fault. Questions are overflowing in your mind as you rob yourself of happiness, and you cannot catch your breath because fear is giving you an earful of lies. You must kill the lies by choosing to be happy. Happiness goes a long way. Bring back the flow of happiness.

Slowly but surely, I let the happiness back into my life. There were times when I psyched myself out and let happiness play peek-a-boo as I let despair, pain, hurt, stress, and depression back into my life.

When I had to start from ground zero, I didn't think I was going to make it. I was a fallen warrior who didn't have any armor for protection. All of my weapons of bravery, peace, sanity, and joy were stolen from me. I was abandoned without any protection from the world. I was left with three children to raise on my own, and my youngest only five months old. I was wondering how was I going to survive.

Nowhere was I protected. I was vulnerable, and I thought I didn't have ownership of myself because I couldn't find myself in the multitude of challenges that I was facing alone. I felt like this is the end, because I didn't have the will to fight. My cross was too heavy to bear. The mountains were too steep and slippery to climb. I was straying off track because the roads were uneven. The detours weren't in my favor because I was confused and decisions were too difficult to make. All I could think of was, *please, someone help me!* I, the fallen warrior was weak, fragile, and in those uncertain times, feeling lost and blind. I felt defeated and felt like giving up. Fear took over my mind because all I could think of were my children.

When I looked into my children's eyes, I knew I had three reasons to live. I knew I had three little people to live for. I had to set fire to yesterday and watch it burn as I started a new tomorrow. It was a new day, and the past didn't exist, but the past made me stronger than I ever was before.

I was holding on during the midnight hours as I prayed for strength to discover a new meaning of a new, reborn life. Tomorrow was mine, and I claimed it by surrendering and knowing that the Great Divine was my protection. I surrendered to stress, depression, feeling sick, miserable, angry, and a victim.

No longer was I consumed by being a prisoner in my mind. I was not willing to give in to the cards I was dealt. I took my power back and I had control of the cards, and as I held the cards in my hand, I shuffled them to my liking. I knew I wasn't always going have the best hand every single time, but I knew I had the power to shuffle when I needed to reexamine my hand.

This transformation helped me to become productive and my mindset became focused on change for the better. My identity was the essence of me, and the path without fear was ahead of me as I walked, knowing that happiness, grace, joy, and love were my birthright!

I might have been left with three children, but I was in the transition of making things happen. I gave myself permission to be open to a new path of freedom. I was open to how I wanted my life to be and how I wanted to feel. Every day I awoke with a passion, and that passion gave me a purpose.

You do not have to accept the approval of others. Honestly, who gives a shit, because their lives are messed up, too. They are always going to judge because they are keeping an eye on your accomplishments. Therefore, they are always going to have something to talk about because you are doing something right.

You look at your life and ask, *why are they so jealous; I do not have anything they want*. Oh, yes ma'am you have everything they want. And it starts with who you are as a person. They want to be you.

They want your strength.

They want your courage.

They want your confidence.

They want your stride.

And they want your joy.

One might say, it's easier said than done. Of course, I have been down that road as well. I agree one hundred percent that it's so much easier said than done. I am very much aware that life sometimes is like tossing a coin in the air calling heads or tails, but it doesn't matter what side it lands on; life goes on.

It is hard when you've lost the will to fight because you've been fighting for so long. You are smothered by the pain. Mentally, you are drained. Physically, you are weak. Emotionally, you are weighed down. Spiritually, you do not have one tiny mustard seed of faith. The common denominator is that other people's problems have clouded your mind with all of their negativity. You cannot feel anything; you are numb. You do not have the energy to surrender, and you choose not to escape because you feel safe when you are closed in.

As you move throughout the day, you do just enough to get by. Your mindset has changed from giving it your all to—well, something is better than nothing. You move in slow motion like a zombie, and there isn't any color, just black and white, with every now and then a shade of gray. You've shut everyone out and crawled back into the rabbit hole. Life passes you by as you feel like you cannot go on.

You look around for help; for someone to take the pain away and to share your suffering, but no one is there. You feel alone, you drift away when you glance ahead and see that there are more uphill battles ahead of you. You do not have the option to turn around because all of the roads are blocked.

You stand exactly where you are without making a step. You try to think of something, but you are emotionally bankrupt.

Where do you go from here? You do not have a clue.

Standing still isn't helping because you've welcomed unwanted visitors; voices are in your head, asking, "What are you waiting for? Take the leap. Jump." They go on to say, "You've had enough. Your burdens are too heavy."

You walk towards the cliff; you turn your head and look at the steep hill towards the mountain. The view isn't helping; not only do you have to climb the steep hill, but you have to climb up the mountain too.

You take a step; rocks and dust fall off the cliff. You stumble and you move forward. The voices in your head call you a coward. You are beginning to second-guess yourself because you want to throw in the towel. You close your eyes; a tear falls and travels to your chin. As your eyes are closed the Great Divine's voice is louder; yet, calmer, soothing; and you feel peace instantly. Your mind feels light, and your body feels balanced. The Great Divine whispers gently and softly in your ear:

"Fallen Warrior, I know you have given everything you've got, and you feel like you have nothing left to give.

Fallen Warrior, I know it's been a while since you smiled.

Fallen Warrior, I see that you are hurting, and I feel your pain.

Fallen Warrior, this is not the end. This is the start of your new beginning.

Fallen Warrior, do not doubt My or your abilities; you have more going for you than you have going against you.

Fallen Warrior, keep moving, you have what it takes; perseverance is your middle name.

Fallen Warrior, you are not the victim! You are the victor!

You step back because you know why you are here. You know why you are alive. Sometimes you have to be your own Shero.

I was a sophomore in college when I received a letter in the mail saying I was no longer eligible for financial aid. I was very concerned because my life circumstances weren't working out in my favor. It was one thing after another. A month or two earlier, my husband (who is now my ex-husband) visited his family up north for Thanksgiving and had never returned. I worked hard to prepare for the upcoming term. I finally found a reasonable in-home daycare babysitter for my little one. I registered for classes that worked around my children's school schedule. Although I was going through hard times, I was mentally prepared to take on the task that was set before me.

The very next day, I went to see my financial aid counselor; she told me there wasn't anything she could do to help. I sat in my car and cried until my paper was soaked. I had to get myself together because I had to pick my children up from school.

Later that night, I wrote in my journal, and I came across a statement I'd written a while back. It said: *No Cross, No Crown.* So, I asked the Great Divine to help me because I had to graduate from college.

The next day, I was on a mission. I called a nearby school that was down the street from the school I was attending. I applied to that school and I was accepted. I was approved for financial aid as well. I attended the nearby school full-time. I used my refund check to pay for the previous school I was attending and took classes there too. I worked as a work-study student at the nearby school. It all worked out in my favor—the previous school was on quarters, and the nearby school was on semesters.

I had the perfect schedule and I managed to pick up my children on time from after-school care. I made sure I spent time with my babies, cooked dinner, and helped them with their homework. After bath and devotion, it was my "me" time—I pulled a lot of all-nighter's because I had to keep up my grades at both schools. But I was rocking it!

There were times when I came up short with my utility bills. I had to squeeze in time to take classes at a non-profit organization to receive assistance. I used that time wisely. I multitasked after I completed their assignments; I used the extra time to complete my homework and/or study.

During the process of taking care of my responsibilities, attending two schools, working, and attending a class to receive assistance with my utilities, I received a notice stating my house was going into foreclosure. I was given a certain amount of time to move out. Thankfully, my application was accepted for an income-based apartment. It wasn't the best, but I couldn't complain. We had somewhere to stay.

I had my share of struggles and yes, I was a fallen warrior, but each day I had to make the best of it or give up and have nothing. I refused to work so hard and have nothing to show for it. I was determined to continue the journey. During my journey, there were days when I walked so slowly because I was dead tired. There were also days when I was tired, but I had an upbeat pace because I knew I had to train my mind to suck it up, get it done, and make it through another day. There were many days I really wanted to stay in bed, but that wasn't an option. I had to keep moving in order to accomplish my goal—which was to stick to the plan because I had worked too hard not to graduate college.

Within a year or so, I managed to bring my GPA up at the previous school, and the following year I walked across the stage with my Bachelor's degree in Biology!

As a fallen warrior, you are human; and you have your moments. There are days when you have more ups than downs, and some days you have more downs than ups. I most definitely can relate.

I was floating through life, but I had to change my mindset. During my worst days, I felt horrible, and when I started to think negatively I felt like I was dishonoring myself. I felt sick, I felt afraid, fear began to control my every move. I felt like demons were trying to break in and take over my life.

One particular night, I tossed and turned. I felt so uncomfortable, but I knew I couldn't afford to lose any sleep. I got up and checked on my children. They were sleeping peacefully. I sat at the table in the dark. Thinking. I had so much on my mind because I didn't have any room for error.

My eyes were heavy. I walked back into my room and laid down. Instead of lying on my left side; I decided to lie on my back. I closed my eyes, and a couple of hours later I felt a presence. I quickly opened my eyes and saw a dark spirit draped in black. It flew around me. I couldn't believe my eyes. I thought I was dreaming, but it was real. It had a creepy smile without any teeth; its voice sounded oily, and it asked me slowly, "Do you want me to come in?" I had a cross on a chain around my neck, but I was paralyzed. I couldn't feel anything. I couldn't move. I couldn't make a sound. I tried to yell for help, but no words came out of my mouth.

I felt more pressure; and it asked me again, "Do you want me to come in?" I had to shut down my fears and I said in my head over and over again, "*The Lord is my Shepherd. The Lord is my Shepherd. The Lord is my Shepherd. The Lord is my Shepherd.*"

I do not recall how many times I said it, but the more I repeated the *Lord is my Shepherd,* I felt the weight lifting and the voice of the dark spirit fading away. I saw it rise above my body and it flew out of the window. I sat up. I was breathing so hard. I said, "Thank you, God!" I ran to see if my children were okay. They were sleeping. I stayed awake for the rest of the night.

The next day, I was tired. I slept through the day as my children took a nap. When night arrived, my mindset was different from the previous night. I was filling my mind with positive thinking, and positive affirmations were rolling off my tongue. I had the power, and I was in control.

Fallen warriors, you might fall, but you are like eagles! You work effortlessly as you soar high into the clouds. You ride the winds of change as you gather all of your strength, courage, and patience. You develop wisdom during your challenges of transformation while you tear down your boundaries one obstacle at a time.

Dear Fallen Warrior, you will not fall apart. Not all wars are meant to have weapons. Your armor is your mind, peace, happiness, drive–and your life. You are powerful! You are unique! You are a warrior because you are the chosen one!!

AFFIRMATION

Take the healing that is being offered. Untangle your fears. Confidence and perseverance are your purposes.

Side Effects

It is important to keep one foot in front of the other. As a woman, you have to fake it until you make it. There will be a lot of twists and turns. There will be mountains that are steep and seem to be too high to climb. However, where there's a will, there's a way. Giving up isn't an option.

Never-ending obstacles pile up one after another. The process seems to repeat itself over and over again without a solution. You've been here before. Where does it end? *When* does it end? Things seem to stay the same or they become worse than before. How many times do you have to compromise? You cannot continue to carry everyone's burdens and their side effects as if everything is just fine.

Not only do you carry the side effects of others, but their side effects are contagious. This affects you mentally to the point where you lose yourself in the process of trying to fix a situation or a person that is beyond repair.

You find yourself helping others who solely depend on you for their mental state and their ability to think for themselves. Foolishly, you do not see how often you carry their burdens. Their side effects begin to poison your life.

It becomes a hazard because this sucks the life out of you, and you begin to neglect yourself, but they do not care. As long as you are doing for them and supplying their needs, they are fine. Their faces are the same on a daily basis, but the person you do not recognize is yourself. Their side effects begin to make you sick, yet you ignore the signs. The warning signs have been there for years, but again, you push yourself because you feel like someday soon you will finally make them happy.

There were plenty of times when I had long restless nights from the side effects I had to carry because of people's selfish ways. I had my share of bitter days when I was left to take care of my family alone. When I needed a helping hand, the only hand I saw reaching out to me was my own. The people who I'd helped extended their negative energy and waited for me to fail.

It is a given that you loved hard but you didn't get the love you deserved in return. The work you put in was beyond brilliant, but it went unnoticed. Instead, you received a litany of side effects that would wear off with time.

Nothing is the same. Everything has changed and life has taken a turn for the worse. Side effects are making you sick. Sick of life. Sick of struggling.

The side effects take a toll on you. You feel yourself trembling, and it is unbearable to breathe and think about what's next. You begin to slip into the deep end and feel numb. Your thoughts drift as the side effects get closer and closer to the point that you want to give up. The more and more they pull you underneath you can't help but think, *I do not have any fight left in me.*

Wake-up call! You have a lot to lose. You have more fight in you than you ever knew. You didn't give yourself the opportunity to love yourself. You didn't give yourself the ability to live and love life. You have given so much to others. Imagine, if you gave to yourself what you've given to others, what life would be like. Do not get lost in the deep end. You have to live for the *now*. Believe it or not, everything will fall into place. It doesn't look like it at the moment, but better days lie ahead.

You are learning that what you see is not what you get, because people live in their own fantasy world until the truth is exposed. Once the truth is exposed they cannot surrender or escape. However, you can surrender and heal from their side effects. The damage can be repaired. You think that you are caught in a bad dream. No, pinch yourself, it is real, and it is giving you the ability to open your eyes to the reality of life.

For far too long you turned a blind eye, but the damage is done. However, you do not have to lose a part of yourself in the process. The broken pieces of your aching heart and damaged emotions can be fixed. You didn't see it coming, or maybe you did. Either way, it has happened. There is nowhere to run or hide from the side effects. Call them out! Suit up and face them head-on because you are a survivor.

Either let the side effects eat you alive from the inside out, or face the truth and make the best of it. The choice is yours.

When it rains, it pours but that isn't a bad thing. Take advantage of the rain as it washes away all of the residues that the side effects left behind. As you confront your side effects, walk with pride, do not turn back, face them head-on. Nothing can faze you now because the rain is clearing your path. After the rain has washed away the side effects, their powers are watered down. Therefore, they can no longer interrupt your peace, kill your joy or steal your happiness.

The side effects' time has expired. It is time to put an end once and for all to carrying everyone's dirty load. Leave them where they lie. Let them figure out their own messes and bad decisions.

Take a breather and let it go. I bet the load is so much lighter!

Now that you have eliminated the side effects that drown your thoughts, you can heal them from within. I noticed that during the day I was okay; my darkest hours came when night fell and I had time on my hands to think. As I begin to think too long, I started to think wrong. I became my worst critic. I had to train my mind to use my negative thoughts to spread and light up my confidence. I became strong-willed as I focused on accomplishing my goals.

As my thoughts chased the hurt and the pain, I found myself smiling because I no longer had a home anymore for the side effects that once wounded my heart. I was in a place of recovery. Self-assurance healed my heart as it beat for me.

Therefore, you have to train your mind to turn negative thoughts into positive ones. When you think about the bad side effects from before, you have to look back on how far you've come. I bet you are proud of yourself!

The cure has taken place. You've created a thicker skin in the process. You've humbly put everyone's burden on the wayside because it is not your shit—nor it is your problem. Once upon a time when you were sinking as they watched, as they thought you were drowning, you found the strength to kick your legs, make progress, and the tide gave you the push you needed to hold your head just above the water. You took your first breath of a new birth and a new life.

Acceptance of others is not your priority anymore. They hate to see you winning so they call you the weakest link, make up lies and are filled with envy. Laughing is good for your soul; therefore, you laugh, because their backbiting isn't painful any longer, nor can it leave marks because their venom is watered down.

As I cured myself, I couldn't believe the limitations I'd allowed people to put on me. I felt the pain cut me deep; the scars are my proof of survival. I felt myself trying to please everyone. During this time, it helped me realize that I would have been spending a lifetime trying to please people who would never be satisfied. Goodness gracious, there is no way I could have been the solution to everyone's problems. After I put everyone's burdens down I was called the weakest link. I was happy knowing I was living up to my standards and finally finding myself.

As I happily gathered my thoughts, I wondered why people would put so much pressure and responsibility on one person? Do they not have consciences? It is incredible how people can make someone that is helping them feel defeated, lost and confused.

You have to realize it is impossible to be the shero to everyone. There comes a time when you have to make a difficult decision to say no to the ones you love. If not, you will be fighting a never-ending battle that you will lose every time. Sad but true, you have to be cruel to be kind, otherwise, you will be defeated.

When I was younger, my sisters and I spent many nights at my aunt's house. She had a heart of gold, and she was such a loving person. My aunt owned a daycare, and she helped so many people without asking for anything in return. She was an angel on earth and blessed so many people.

My aunt took time out and asked all of her nieces and nephews what we wanted for Christmas. During Christmas, we had a gathering at her house. That's how thoughtful she was. However, as I became older and wiser, I noticed all the things she did for people. I sometimes wonder, was her kindness being taken for granted and was that the cause of her death?

There were people in my family who always had their hands out, asking my aunt for this and that. It was as if my aunt was an ATM machine. To this day, I do believe my aunt would be alive and well today if she hadn't had to carry everyone's side effects. She was everyone's solution until she became sick with cancer. She has now been deceased for more than two decades. Everyone who wanted handouts from her is still alive and well; they figured out how to pay their bills, solve their money issues, and moved on in life.

When I look back at my aunt's memory—she always wanted grandchildren. I wish she was here to enjoy the life she worked hard for and deserved.

When the side effects knock you down, find the strength to get up because you are a soldier. You've paid your dues, and nobody can hurt you because your foundation is solid.

You are not broken down anymore. The Grim Reaper cannot steal your joy. You are no longer its victim. You are victorious, feeling good and living free! The 'treatment' gave you a turbocharge to find a cure. The cure is to love yourself more and to put yourself first.

You've lived and learned that timing is everything. Time is precious. Your birthright is happiness, love, peace, and joy. As you travel the road of life, you now know when to pay attention. You now know your worth, and as you walk down the path without fear, you are learning more and more about yourself than you have ever known. No matter how old you are—you are learning the fundamentals of life forces that will help guide you along the way. You are learning that there's no need for a flashlight because the love you have for yourself is shining so brightly that everyone notices as you walk past them.

Doesn't it feels good that you broke free, broke the leash and there is no stopping you? The miracle of change is all about focusing on yourself by tuning-up your mind, body, soul, and spirit.

Tell yourself, *I know why I am here. I know why I am alive.* Be honest with yourself and be open to how you want your life to feel. Feeling new, refreshed and learning how to love again. You deserve to smile.

All the pain was wearing you down. The battles left you shattered and broken. There were times you were stumbling, but you didn't fall. Each tear you cried brought you to this moment. Your scars gave you strength to heal, and they taught you how to love and appreciate yourself.

You rose above it all!

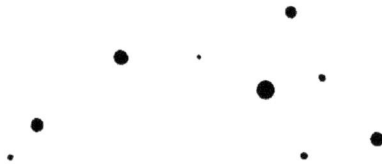

AFFIRMATION

"Another one bites the dust. I am reaping the benefit of self-fulfillment and self-control. I am worthy of all the good things in life."

Loved and Lost

As a woman, you walk into all kinds of unknown situations that cause you to fall in love, put someone else's needs before your own, and make unbelievable sacrifices. As time goes by, falling in love has its consequences. You fall in love with your mate, children, family, and job. However, you do not receive a fraction of what you have given in return. Sadly, nobody sees you are beyond exhausted. They want you to go, go and go without complaining.

If they carefully pay attention and think about it; when was the last time they saw you smile, truly smile? When was the last time they saw you happy, truly happy? When was the last time they offered to help you, as opposed to asking could you do this or that? When was the last time they gave you a moment to breathe?

As you work so hard and give so much of yourself, you think things will finally line up. However, that is not the case. Once you set someone up to help them prosper, things in your life start to crumble, and slowly but surely you begin to feel violated. Your hard work is soon forgotten as they drop you where you stand.

Life isn't fair and it is hard. It's even harder when you love so hard and lose so much. You are not perfect. You have your flaws, and most definitely you have your moments. However, you have a good heart and you try to treat others how you want to be treated. Time and time again you give people all of your heart by trying to be loving and understanding.

You've learned that when it comes to some people, nothing would ever be good enough. You have to be willing to accept that you loved them to the best of your ability, and only lost someone who caused you to lose more of yourself. Those people aren't worth saving because the question is, who will save you?

However, the love you gave wasn't in vain; it helped you to become a better person. The loss opened your eyes to see that you deserve so much better. It is alright to cry. You are finding your strength and you are beginning to find the voice within. You are special. You are unique. You are loved. There's no need to be afraid. Life is a journey! You will make it. It's okay to let go of the loss and count it all pure joy!

When I was married, I loved my husband. I thought he was too good to be true. I loved how he respected his mother. I was in love with how he valued "family." However, I learned a lot during my journey in the "married" world. There is a lot of giving and taking. Over the years, who I thought I was faded into the background.

My character was tested because I didn't think I would have to compromise so much of who I was as a person. I changed so much because I gave so much of me and lost myself in the process. Sadly, when I lost myself, I did not notice. It just happened; it was more of a habit I formed to adjust. I was damaged from the inside out because my life wasn't mine anymore. I was someone I *had* to be; not who I *wanted* to be. I wasn't someone that made "me" happy. I made everyone else happy, and it wasn't enough.

Losing yourself is scary.

When I first met my ex-husband, he was a property manager at the apartments where I was residing at that time. I moved into a new apartment complex, not knowing he was living there. He put a letter on my door telling me how much he was attracted to me. I ignored him because I wasn't interested in dating. I was single for about two years and I was happy being alone. A friend of mine at the time suggested that I should give him a chance (friends will get your ass in a hot mess, then leave!). After leaving two or three letters on my door, he also left his number. I called after a month or so, and it took off from there.

He was very respectful, loving, and kind. What stood out the most was the fact that I loved how he respected his mother.

As time went on, we became a couple, and it was a serious relationship.

He took a position in Alabama and I helped him move. My children, who were two and six years old (who aren't his biological children) and I traveled to Alabama every other weekend. Most of the time, it was every weekend because he had to work.

Loving him, I thought I couldn't get any higher and I knew that it was love and he was "the one." I made many mistakes. My first mistake was, my grandmother used to say, if a man loves you more than you love him, that is better than you loving him more than he loves you. I felt like he loved me more than I loved him, and I settled because he "loved" me more.

There were signs I noticed, but I never paid any attention to because I felt as though it was "normal." I noticed I had to compromise more than I should. If he wanted to do something, more than likely I would give in and say okay. If I didn't compromise, we would argue. However, I didn't think it would become a huge problem in the future. I really thought that in a relationship we all have to compromise one way or another. Therefore, I felt like my emotions were wrong.

When I visited his family for the first time, I felt content and welcomed by some of his family members. More so, his Pops, his uncles, aunties, brother, and extended family. His mother was warm, but just like every mother she was cautious, and that was fine.

However, she said something to me that I will never forget. She said, "You've changed my boy." I thought she was saying I'd changed him for the better. No. She was saying I changed him for the worse because he didn't smoke or drink with her anymore.

When I met him, I told him that I would not allow myself to be involved with someone who smoked or drank. It was a lesson learned from my past relationship and I wasn't willing to settle for what I did not want. My ex-husband made the decision to stop smoking and drinking. I didn't tell him to—I simply told him what I wasn't going to settle for.

I should have taken what his mother said at face value. It was never my intention to change him; I just wasn't going to settle for what I didn't want. I knew that I'd been there, done that, and I wasn't going to do that again.

When he met my family, my mother welcomed him with open arms. My siblings did too, but my oldest sister is very protective and she never, ever, gets along with anyone. She told me, "Nobody is that perfect. He is hiding something." I thought was she jealous and I didn't take what she said seriously.

My daddy said, "Baby girl, his true colors will come out sooner rather than later, because there's something about him, but I cannot put my finger on it. If you are happy, then I am happy as well." I thought my daddy was being protective of his baby girl, but I should have listened.

That was another sign or two. I should have listened because people who have your best interests at heart can see better from the outside looking in.

Years passed, and we had a great relationship! We always did things together as a family. We would go to church every Sunday and sometimes on Wednesdays. During the evening, we would more than likely be at his job because he was managing two properties when he moved back to Georgia. Things were perfect.

I noticed things changed when I stopped compromising more than usual. It took a toll on me because that was when many of our arguments took place. I would always give in because I was tired of arguing. To hear him tell it, he said I was the one who controlled the relationship. He said, "I never dated a woman who wore the pants because I was always in control." I felt like he was saying I should let him make all the decisions. He knew when he met me that I was an outspoken person who thought for herself. I was surprised he would even make that statement because a woman has a voice too.

I felt like we could have worked through it. After all, nobody is perfect. I felt as though he was going to accept me – flaws and all – and vice-versa. I must say again, my emotions were counterfeit, and my opinion didn't matter as long as he was happy.

I didn't think I wore the pants; I was just being the person who I knew best and that was me. Our relationship turned sour because as he would say I didn't know how and when to wear a skirt. He would always say I never let him be a man.

I talked to my daddy and asked him, "How do I let a man be a man?" I went into great detail and told my daddy that my fiancé at that time said I didn't know how to wear a skirt because I always wore the pants and I never let him be a man. How do I let him be a man?

I continued and said, "I let him lead the way. At times, I step aside and let him be the man. I cook, clean, take care of the household, and I am very supportive. I don't know what else to do."

My daddy asked me was I a man or a woman? I said I am a woman! He said, "Right, therefore, he has to know how to be a man." He went on to say, "That is something you are taught at a young age, and with some men, they learn it as they grow in a relationship or marriage."

My ex-husband's father passed when he was young, but he had his Pops in his life. As time passed, I figured out who was part of the problem. Honestly, it was his mother.

When we had our issues, our biggest mistake was telling people about the problems in our marriage. However, we had to talk to someone or we would have bitten each other's head off. My grandmother told us before we got married to never tell anyone about your business. She said, "If it gets too hot in the front, damn it, take your ass to the back, and if it gets too hot in the back then take your ass back to the front. Never tell anyone your business."

I talked to my family and he talked to his. I never thought his mother liked me in the first place, which was fine; I have a lot of people who don't like me, and that's their issue. Life goes on.

Before we got married, we went to marriage counseling. One of the pastors said, "Charlena, I do not think he is ready to leave his mother. He thinks he is ready for marriage, but he isn't ready to leave his mother." Although she lived miles away up north, he clung to his mother's every word.

During our wedding rehearsal, his mother preferred not to participate and she stayed at her hotel. That was a sign within itself.

Two days before the wedding, a friend texted me and he asked me not to get married. He said I was supposed to marry him. I texted him back and told him he'd had his chance. My fiancé at the time asked me who was I texting—I lied and told him, my sister, because he would have taken everything out of context. He read the messages and stormed out of the house. I didn't talk to him for an entire day. I didn't know where he was, nor did I know if the wedding was going to take place.

I was wrong for lying, but I knew if I had told him the truth, he wouldn't have taken it lightly. Either way, it was a lose-lose situation, and I should have told him the truth. I talked to my mom about it. I sat in my car and banged on my steering wheel because it was a disaster.

My auntie told me to put my heart in my pocket and think with my head.

I didn't want to waste money, not to mention my grandmother was always in my ear saying, "Y'all need to get married. Y'all carrying on around here playing house."

I was under so much pressure. All of the signs were right in my face and I ignored everything, trying to make everyone happy but me.

Needless to say, when I got out of the horse carriage for the wedding my brother said, "Big sis, are you sure you want to do this?" That was the most important question of my life. I wasn't sure. I wasn't ready, but I did it anyway.

After we got married, we had more bad days than good.

The problem was, he would always let his mother disrespect me. He never corrected her. He would say, "She is my mother, and you are my wife, and I am not going to disrespect my mother."

I told him the love of a mother and a wife are totally different.

He didn't understand.

My oldest sister had one time, and one time only, to disrespected my husband. I checked her and told her she did not have to like him, but one thing was for sure when he was in her presence she had to respect him. I never had an issue with her after that.

Unlike my sister, my husband's mother always talked to me any kind of way; and he let her. That's what destroyed our marriage, along with other things.

During our marriage, we just about lived at his office as he was the manager of three apartment buildings. After picking the kids up from school every day, we went to his office. During the weekends we went to the office so he would catch up on paperwork. After church, guess what? We went to his office! I always helped him because he took on too much, even though I was going to school and taking care of my family. However, nothing was ever good enough.

Sometimes it is the smallest things that count. Such as, I wanted him to say, "Babe, the house smells good and it is so clean!" or "Thank you, Babe, for working so hard. I really appreciate your help with everything." Or once in a while, "Thank you, Babe, for dinner, running my bathwater and ironing my clothes." It would have been nice to hear, "Thank you so much, Babe. I don't know how I can do all of this without you." However, nothing was good enough, and more and more was expected from me without appreciation.

I wasn't perfect in my marriage. I had my time as well when I was cold or cruel—because I was tired! I was tired of not feeling appreciated.

I was tired of his mother always saying, "You are in school while my son is slaving and working his ass off." She didn't know what the hell I had to go through and she wasn't making it any better.

I went to school because I wanted to bring a decent share of income into the house as well. I didn't want him to carry the load alone.

I became bitter and begin to lose respect for him. I will admit I had a smart mouth because I was tired of always being blamed by his mother for everything that went wrong. I was tired of the one-sided stories.

I begin to give only a percentage of myself—what was the point in working so hard? It wasn't noticed, nor was it appreciated.

I was pregnant with my youngest son, and I said things out of bitterness and hurt. He was supposed to be named after my husband and his family – he would be the IV, but instead, I gave my son his own name. I told my husband, "If you want a son to have your name, go have another son by someone else." I knew I was wrong, but I felt like he disrespected me by not speaking up for me, for his mother was always right and she always had the last say-so—as if she ran our marriage. She might have run his ass but she for damn sure didn't tell me what to do!

After I gave birth to my son, his mother and Pops visited. I wasn't at the house to greet them when they arrived, I was at my grandmother's. My grandmother said, "Baby, hold your head up and head on home. You are a wife now and his family is your family. I know his mother is a piece of work, God bless her heart, but you have to face her and be respectful. After all, she is his mother."

I laid my head on my grandmother's knee and asked, "Grandma, what did I get myself into?"

She replied, "You cannot dwell on that now, for it is done, and you have to take it as it comes. Make sure you welcome them in your home and ask God for strength."

When I arrived home, I sat in the car for a minute or two. I asked God to give me strength and I walked through the door. I had a smile on my face but of course, it was forced.

I didn't want to hug that lady, but my grandmother's voice was in my head. I asked her how she and Pops were doing and how was the drive.

They answered fine and good.

Pops and I talked more than usual.

I asked my husband's mother did she want to hold my son, who was maybe three months old. She held him, and she looked at him. I wanted to say, "Yes, he's your son's child," but I didn't say anything. I just said to myself, *God give me strength because I do not want to go to jail because I may strangle this lady tonight.*

As I was fixing my little one's bathwater. I heard her say, "Oh no, someone come get this baby, he is shitting all over me." I wanted to kick her ass out of my house! Instead, I told my husband to get my baby.

Later that evening, she made a smart-ass comment, "I do not like this house." How could she not? We'd just bought the house in December. Okay, whatever. I let that slide. Additional comments she made were uncalled for. She said she didn't like the sheets on the bed. I didn't know why not, because they were brand new.

Before they arrived, I made sure their rooms were tidy and very comfortable. The house was spick and span (like always because I am a clean person and always have been).

I told myself to ignore her ass since she would never be satisfied because she didn't like me. I believe she didn't like me because first, I was in school, and second because her son was married. She had two sons and both of them were married.

Their stay was only for three days, but goodness, I felt like she stayed for three decades!

I was so happy that she was leaving, I smiled (a real smile this time around) and wished them the best and a safe trip back.

One month passed.

One day, my husband was offered a higher position. I told him not to take it because we had enough on our plate. After he talked to his mother, he took his eyes off the prize, which was peace in our home, and accepted the position. He let money and his mother rule over us being comfortable and financially stable.

She called me and told me that I was a selfish bitch.

I wasn't selfish. I just knew that we, as a family, couldn't bite off more than we could chew. I was always taught that I shouldn't ever live beyond my means.

After he took the position, things went downhill faster than a car without brakes. Our house was a hell hole day and night.

Less than a month later, he was laid off because he couldn't live up to what the company wanted him to do. It was too much on us because we never had time to enjoy life. We were always at work, work, work. The kids slept on an air mattress at his job because we lived there day in and day out, every single day.

He went into a state of depression. He laid on the living room floor, balled up, as his tears fell on the pages of his Bible. I comforted him as much as I could, as I tried to be positive and productive at all times. I had to take on the responsibility of taking care of the household as he laid on the floor for almost a month.

I was worn down physically. Emotionally, I was drained, but I didn't have time to focus on how I felt. I had to use any and every bit of energy for my family.

When I was in Endocrinology, his mother called me and told me that my husband was texting everyone saying that he was going to kill himself. She didn't make matters any better. She told me if he killed himself that I should always remember that it was my fault. She called me a selfish bitch and everything that comes after and before that.

I was overwhelmed with so much. I went straight to the house. As I walked in the door, he was lying on the floor, crying. Every day the house smelled like musk because he didn't want to bathe. I held him in my arms and told him he was loved, wanted, and we needed him.

I carried more on my back because I had to keep a watch on him at all times. Every Tuesday and Thursday for a couple of weeks, I went to my mother's job to fax off his resumes. During the evening, after I put the kids to bed, I would send his resumes off to different companies by e-mail. I would form an assembly line on my dinette table, prepare his resumes and send them off by postal as well.

As time went on it wasn't about me or my needs—it was about what I needed to do for my family. I lost myself somewhere about a year ago, and I never got "me" back.

Needless to say, I failed most of my classes.

My days were never-ending and I didn't have time to rest. I felt like I wasn't human because it was impossible for me to keep moving without resting.

Everything I did wasn't good enough, because all I heard him say was—my momma said this. My momma said. One night, he stormed out of the house to stay with his best friend because I asked him to get my little one because he was crying. I was so tired I couldn't move. He just laid there. When I got up, that's when he got up. I yelled and hit him on the leg and said, "I got it!"

He stormed out of the house. His mother called me and said I beat her son. I couldn't entertain that lady because I was too damned tired for that shit.

There was no way I had strength or energy to beat him when I was constantly on the move; helping him, taking the kids to and from school, going to school as well, and working a part-time job. Not to mention, I was cooking, cleaning and everything else that came with being a wife and mother.

After he left to stay with his friend, I was all alone raising my children. I was alone trying to put the scraps together. Mentally, it was a struggle. While he was at his friend's house playing games, I was trying to keep up with the next second and preparing for what it was going to hold.

A month passed. He came home, and as soon as he set foot in the door he said, "I am going to visit my family up north." I was speechless because he'd been gone for a month, and he was coming home to pack and leave again. I asked him when he was coming back. He said, "I am going up there for a few days. Just for Thanksgiving."

I packed his clothes; and needless to say, he never came back. Months went by, and I asked him to come back home. I told him we could go to counseling and fix things. I waited for a year. He said he was coming back when he was ready.

I came to my senses and realized I was being sold a dream. No more was I going to play the fool by lying to myself. I had to wake up because my bags were heavy; I had filled my bags with lies and false hopes, and they weighed me down. I had to put down each bag because they were his way of making me believe in sweet nothing.

All that I sacrificed wasn't good enough. My love wasn't good enough. My support wasn't good enough. My actions weren't good enough. Nothing was good enough. However, I knew I had to weather the storm, not give up, and suit up for what was to come.

I thought I'd lost control of my life. It was a nightmare! Every time I came up for air, the stress and weight from his lies and my fooling myself pulled me back underwater. I was drowning, lifeless. I lost myself, my soul was hurting and aching from suffering every single day.

I found the strength to carry on. I couldn't let the situation break me down anymore. I was better than that. I might not have been good enough for him; my loyalty, support, and dedication weren't to his liking. That was okay. I didn't need approval from anyone.

I'd been fighting for so long, and the one thing that I thought I'd lost was never gone.

I loved myself!

I knew that my love was good enough for me.

I had loved and lost, but I had found something better—a new, improved, and unstoppable me!

Your husband needs you to be at his beck and call as you take care of your home, children, and responsibilities at work. You humbly support him the best you can. However, what you have done is not good enough; more is demanded. As your husband demands more support, the support that you've given is overlooked. Furthermore, you manage to carry the load until you have no fight left. Sadly, what you've done continues to go unnoticed.

You will be constantly thinking; how can I make this better? How can I change? How can I make him happy? How can I give more to the point he is satisfied? How can I love him more? How can I give more of myself? How can I fix it? How can I? is going to be your anthem, and you are going to drive yourself crazy because he's moving on and he will not look back.

Be honest with yourself. You were at your lowest and broken down. You were unsure and lost hope. You were hiding your fears until you showed them on your sleeve. You felt like everything and everyone was the hammer and you were the nail as they were beating down on you, and it was never-ending. Their empty threats had you scared and you were always running because your weakness was exposed. You were their prey. You didn't know who to believe because of their mixed signals.

You might not see it now, but you are stronger than you can ever imagine.

You cannot become comfortable in your pain. You have to let the pain that you feel turn you into a rose without thorns. There are sixteen pieces on the chessboard. The king is the most important piece, but the difference is that the queen is the most *powerful* piece!

You are a queen, you can maneuver around your opponents; they do not have the power over your life, your mind or soul. You might think you've been a prisoner, but that is your past'. Look in the now and work your way to how you want your future to be. Exercise your thoughts into a pattern of letting go, and think positively about more of what you want than what you do not want.

Queen!

You are a queen! As a matter of fact, you are *the* queen! Act as if you know it!

You are powerful, determined, strong, and you can make the biggest and most extravagant move and put it into action.

Lights, camera, strike a pose and own it!

It is yours to own!

Yes, you loved and loved so much. You also lost as well, but you lost hurt, pain, agony, and confusion. You've lost interest in wanting to know answers to unanswered questions. You've lost the willingness to give a shit about what others think. You've surrendered to being fine, that you cannot change the things you have no control over.

You've lost a lot, but you've gained closure. You are now balanced, centered, focused, and filled with peace surrounding you in your heart, mind, body, and soul.

Your pride was hurt, but you would rather walk alone and be more willing to give and learn more about the queen you are.

You lost yourself in the process, but the more you learn about the new you, the more you will be so much in love with yourself. The more you learn about the new you, the more you will know your worth. The more you learn about the new you, the happier you are going to be, and this time around you will be smiling inside and out!

The dots are now connecting. You feel alive!

You know now that all is not lost. Now that you've cut the cord it is time to give your heart a second chance at loving yourself.

Silence your mind. Take a deep breath and close your eyes. As you open your eyes, look at your reflection in the mirror. Aren't you beautiful, Queen? Embrace who you are. Smile, laugh, welcome the new you and say,

"My world is just now beginning."

AFFIRMATION

"Queen! You are powerful! Act like you know it!"

Ripple Effect

Awoman lives under pressure on a daily basis. Nearly every day a woman is being criticized for the way she looks, thinks, acts, how she raises her children, and her role in the workplace. She is criticized by other women, her husband and/or significant other, her children, family, and friends. Goodness, gracious, when will a woman's love ever be good enough?

She's constantly beaten down by being told what she's doing wrong, and barely hears what she has done right. Needless to say, she isn't praised for her accomplishments; often, all she hears is criticism. I would love to see the detractors walk in her shoes for a while.

There are times when a woman's plans don't go according to plan because things pop up out of nowhere like a Jack-in-the-Box; and most of the time they aren't in her favor. However, she manages to get them done without hesitation.

I do not know how many times I've played the fool to appease other people when things went wrong. The end result? I was the one who was the jackass.

When I'd had enough of my kindness being taken for weakness, I felt like I was floating in the ocean. People's actions toward me were like the crashing of the waves. Their words and actions were like tides that took me further and deeper into the deep. I didn't have anything to hold on to but the flow of the water kept me afloat. When the tides took me further out, I floated on my back and went with the flow. The water became my friend as it taught me not to panic in trying times.

When I became steady and comfortable people would throw small pebbles. Little did they know, I collected the pebbles because they were so smooth and beautiful. I loved the ripples in the water from the pebbles because they were so peaceful and relaxing.

They noticed the pebble's effect wasn't disrupting my peace. They took it up a notch and cast larger stones and rocks. The ripple effect knocked me off balance. Each cast from a rock bruised my body, so it was hard to stay afloat.

During one of my biggest struggles, the ripple effect was at its worst. I felt as though the ripple was going to turn into a whirlpool – to the point where I thought I was going to drown. My head was under the water and my hands were reaching for something to hold on to. Sadly, there wasn't anyone or anything I could take hold of. However, when I trusted the waves, they carried me to a peaceful place in my mind, to the hidden aspects of my true self where I could explore my options. I had to find comfort in what was given and make the best of it.

Life wasn't easy. Time and time again, it was one battle after another. During the midnight hours, while my children were sleeping, I could see the red dots from gun laser sights crisscrossing the walls of our room. My children and I would sleep together on the floor, hoping and praying we would dodge the bullets that were being fired at our apartment building. It was hell. My heart burned with resentment towards my husband because he had left us to our fate.

I couldn't believe my situation. I thought I was living in a nightmare every single day. However, I wasn't dreaming, I was walking in the reality of my life.

I thought I was going to have a nervous breakdown. I really thought I was going to lose my mind in the process of trying to bounce back.

The ripple effect tried to get the best of me. However, I had to remember how peaceful and relaxing the pebble's ripple effect was. I sat in my closet, wrapped my arms around my legs and as I rocked back and forth, I asked for guidance. I asked The Great Divine, why did He leave me? I asked Him, why? I thought He knew how much I could take.

I laid on the floor in the dark, in tears, asking what I did to deserve such a hell on earth. At that point, my grandmother called me and said God told her to call me, and God told her to tell me to let it go. Let it go. Let it go.

After I got off the phone. I dried my eyes and sat in the closet for a while. I talked to The Great Divine and said, "I am going to suit up and take on the challenges that unfold before me." I was up for the challenge. When I opened the door, I asked The Great Divine to tear down the tower and clear away all of the residues because I am ready to cross the bridge of fear, and I am ready to reach my full potential.

The ripple effect was meant to knock me off balance because the larger stones that were thrown made a bigger splash than intended. That was supposed to defeat me. Ah-ah! Instead, the ripple effect spread wider and made me realize that transformation produces life—and it was up to me what type of life I wanted to produce.

It is up to you if you want to take the leap into happiness, peace, love, and into something new. However, it takes courage. You must allow yourself to heal and start the process of elimination. You have to remember that if you lose yourself, you will lose it all. Life is a series of beginnings and endings. Therefore, letting go doesn't mean you failed; it simply means that time has run out for that particular season in your life.

One ripple effect changed my life for the better. It woke me up! It made me want more, and I worked hard to create the life I wanted for myself and my children. I learned that sometimes when people cast the first stone, they are eager and waiting to see you fail at life. They laugh and giggle because they are happy to see you in fear. They roll on the ground, tickled because they thought you'd lost your power; not realizing they are giving you your power.

The joke's on them.

Never in a million years did they think they were helping you to become a better you! Their ripple effect brought you back to life. You needed that ripple effect because you were sinking deeper and deeper into someone who you weren't. Without the ripple effect, you wouldn't be able to feel the essence of yourself. You know what makes you special; you can hear your own voice. The ripple effect gave you your power back!

When I looked back at this situation, I was bitter. I am good now. My children, nieces and I had a fun day at Six Flags. Shortly after getting something to eat, we got into an accident. A guy hit my car and it was totaled. My mom and sister came to the scene. What got under my skin was that my sister threw a stone (she laughed as if the accident was funny) and it caused a ripple effect.

She laughed because she loved to see someone in a bad situation because misery loves company. I heard her tell her daughters they were going to use the money from the accident to get a car. How self-centered and messed up was that? She didn't care about anyone's well-being; the first thing came to mind was cha-ching! My daughter was injured because the airbag hit her in the face. I thank the Great Divines she turned out to be okay.

While my sister thought that casting the stone by laughing at the situation was going to dampen my mood, I made the ripple effect work to my advantage. I had full insurance coverage, and everything worked out in my favor. I always wanted a Honda Pilot, and that was exactly what I bought. I couldn't have been happier with my purchase. It turned out to be a beautiful ripple effect!

Some people want you to pay it forward, but they overlook the details. They think "paying it forward" is on credit. It's no such thing, and some people think you should pay it forward to *them*. However, they feel like they are not required to return the favor.

Paying it forward means being kind to someone with the hope that they will show kindness to another person in return. That is not always the case. Paying it forward for some people means, "Me. Me. Me. Me." They want to take credit for everything. Not to mention, they act like their shit doesn't stink.

The last two weeks in December 2017, I wrote a letter to my mom, my daddy, and both of my sisters. I hand-wrote two letters for each person. I mailed the letters to them and I set fire to the second copy. I sprinkled sage on the remains, sealed them in a container and took it with me to Myrtle Beach. There, I spread the remains on the beach when the clock struck 12 a.m. on January 1st, 2018. I released the resentment that I'd held inside for so long. I was free, and I must say, it felt so good!

Weeks later, my daddy called me about the letter and we talked. Three months later, my mother and I talked about it face-to-face. My sisters cast a couple of stones because they acted like they didn't care. I'm sure they didn't, but that was okay. I didn't do it for them; I did it for myself.

One of my sisters said I cursed her out and went off on her in the letter, but I do not recall cursing in the letters. I tried to be humble as I got my point across. I wanted them to understand where I was coming from so that we could all work on our flaws in the hope that we could work on our relationships as siblings. I guess the truth really does hurt, and some people do not want to know the truth – they would rather walk in a straight line, not knowing that sooner or later they will have twists and turns in the road. Unexpectedly, there will be sharp curves that will throw them off balance.

We were at Ted's Restaurant. My sisters and I had an awkward moment, but we were casual. The letter came up, and my oldest sister said with a nasty attitude as she tossed her head, "Well, I didn't read the letter."

I looked at her and said, "Oh, okay."

She said, 'Because I didn't care what it said, so I chose not to read it."

As the stones were cast, I handled it well. I felt frustrated because I wanted us to work on becoming closer to how we used to be. I guess I was the only one willing to do so. I am not perfect, but I felt like they had made me feel shitty a hundred times over. When I felt like the time was right, I wanted to express my thoughts. I didn't think I would have offended anyone.

I wasn't offended by my sister's comment. I was hurt, disappointed, and I felt like I was only good enough for what I could do for them and their children. When I needed help, I didn't get it. I helped out my sisters financially more than a couple of times. I was always there for them, no matter what. I was loyal and I felt like my kindness was mistaken for weakness. They never paid it forward in return.

While sitting at the table, I asked my sister how I could change for the better. She was happy to tell me how I could change, but she wasn't willing to read the letter about her flaws. Ummm.

She proudly said with a smirk, "Well… you can stop assuming. You always assume, and you are wrong. Just because you do not see it, doesn't mean it didn't happen."

The first thing came to mind was, who does she think she is, The Great Divine?

I nodded my head, and my oldest son added his two cents and said, "Yeah, Momma is good at assuming."

I added, "I wouldn't have to make assumptions if you were all straightforward with me. If a person isn't direct and honest, then yes, I am going to think what I please. When you ask me a question, you do not have to assume because you are going to receive a direct answer."

My sister looked at me and said, "Well… you asked."

I replied, "I sure did. Thanks for telling me. I will work on it."

She then added, "You think our cousins are better than us, and you put them on a higher pedestal. And I feel really annoyed about that."

I had to collect my thoughts because I wanted to be cordial. My cousins took time out of their busy morning to take me to get surgery at 6 a.m., They were up around 5 a.m. to make sure I got there on time, twice, (I had three knee surgeries). This damaged my relationship with my sisters because the ONE time I really needed them the most they weren't there. They were "too busy."

My cousins showed me they loved me; their actions spoke louder than their words. We formed a tight bond over the years, and my relationship with my sisters faded into the background.

I never understood how my sisters thought that was okay, and everything was supposed to go back to normal. No. I was hurt! I was disappointed! I was sad! I felt like I didn't matter to them.

When I wrote my first book, *No Cross-No Crown: Trust God Through the Battle*, my brother and sister-in-law were the only people in my family who bought my book. My sisters posted it on their social media page and I thank them for that. However, if they had written a book, I would have supported them and bought two or three copies.

My sister said she bought two copies and she wanted me to sign them. I saw her several times and was never offered a copy to sign. That was okay as well!

I couldn't worry about how they felt about the letter. They didn't understand my point of view because I called them out on their actions.

We all have a lot of growing to do. I hope my sisters know that my intentions weren't to make them feel unloved. My letter was meant for change, peace, and for us to come together to work on improving our actions.

If I learned anything that night, I learned that not everyone is willing to change. It's odd. People say they are willing to change but when the time presents itself, are they willing to change or is it just a figure of speech? Because it sounds good?

The ripple effect changes. Eventually, the rings of the ripples change; they either become smaller or wider in length. No matter the size, sooner or later, the ripple will vanish, but the question is—did it leave an effect or was it pointless?

What impact does the ripple effect have on you? Will you reach for great heights, or will you let the ripple effect's "purpose" pass you by?

Their ripple effect didn't affect me because I wrote the letters for ME. I released the resentment that had blocked my life for so many years. For too long, I was smiling in their faces as if everything was fine but my heart was hurting. The sad thing is, nobody noticed, because it was all about what Lena could do for them.

I knew the letters were going to distance us even further, but I had to tell them how I felt. I wasn't going to go into 2018 holding piles of shit on my back.

I decided to choose:

No more sadness because of how someone else will feel.

No more hiding my feelings.

No more avoiding the truth of how I felt.

No more unresolved situations.

No more letting people rob me of my happiness and joy and letting life pass me by.

No more misery and selling myself short.

No more letting people take and steal my inner peace.

No more giving a shit about what other people think of me—they are going to form their opinion anyway—and the question is, who cares? Not me. That's the least of my worries.

No more giving everyone the best of me. It is time for me to fall in love with myself and give myself ALL of me!

The ripple effect was so powerful on my behalf because I felt relieved that I finally knew the true meaning of love and peace, both inside and out.

I only answer to one God and not "man." My life is beautiful, unique and amazing in its own way, and I am happy as I march to the beat of my own rhythm.

The full impact of the ripple effect can at times be unpredictable, but it is what you make of it. It doesn't matter how many stones have been thrown at you because you are the master of your actions. How you view the ripple effect's rings will determine your outcome. Will you let them break you or will you use them to the fullest potential?

As they throw more stones, let them fall where they may. In my opinion, the more rings in the ripple effect the better! Needless to say, they are giving you the opportunity to exchange their hate, backbiting, and negative energy into valuing and loving yourself more. They are helping you create a thicker skin as you find your happiness and you embrace a fruitful future.

This is your moment. You are coming into a time of peace and fulfillment. Take it all in! You put up with a lot of people's shit to get where you are today.

As you evaluate all the amazing ways you've grown and made tremendous progress from all of the stones that were thrown, you can now clearly see your powerful transformation. Your life will be delightful, your heart, soul, and mind will be at peace.

It is your time to experience your adventure and enjoy life!

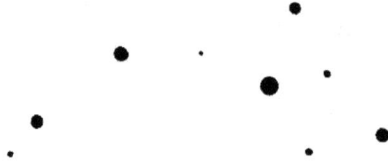

AFFIRMATION

"No more brainwashing—expect the unexpected to blow your mind! Connect with yourself and your life's purpose—then grow.

Self-Fulfillment

A young lady is supposed to be classy, kind, generous, and respectful. She is told she should not display any anger and/or badmouth her peers. A young lady is told to think 'inside the box' and to limit her expectations because her husband will provide for her in the future.

A young lady is taught to never fuss or complain and to always keep a smile on her face. When a young lady speaks her mind, she is told that she is not acting "ladylike."

When a young lady steps out of her comfort zone to challenge herself to fight for what she wants, she is told she is not acting "ladylike."

When a young lady plays a sport, and at times she may be aggressive, she is told that she is not acting "ladylike."

When a young lady is bossy, she is told to humble herself because that is not acting "ladylike." Maybe she isn't bossy, maybe she is confident within herself, has high self-esteem and knows she can dare to be different.

I remembered when my daughter was in middle school. She had her books in her hand, walking to class. A young boy was leaning on the wall, put his foot out and tripped my daughter. She hit the ground hard and fell on her knees; her face almost hit the ground. For some unknown reason, everyone thought it was funny. However, everyone was in a state of shock when my daughter brushed herself off and round-house kicked him in his private parts!

Everyone ran to the young man's rescue. However, there wasn't one person who bothered to ask my daughter if she was okay. There was a teacher who saw the whole thing, yet he defended the young man.

When a young lady no longer plays with baby dolls or toy kitchens, and she's trying to find where she fits in today's society, she is told she needs to learn how to cook, clean, wash, and provide for her husband and family. Why is that so?

Why can't a young lady, learn how to cook, clean and wash clothes so she can learn how to take care of *herself*? It is imperative that a young lady should know how to love and take care of herself first, before she feels she can love and take care of anyone else.

That is where the mistakes begin. A young lady is brought up to put others first. This is when a woman grows up and plays the fool for others because her self-worth was never built on solid ground. Instead, it was built on being a "people pleaser" and putting her life on the back burner.

Consequently, her feelings didn't matter, and her thoughts didn't exist because for so long she was taught to put other people before herself. The question that is never asked is, what happens when a woman (who was once a young lady groomed to give every ounce of herself) loses herself to the point where she has to find a way to dig herself out of the deepest hole? This seems impossible. She doesn't know how because she wasn't ever taught how to express her feelings, troubles, and/or grieve.

The young lady was once a rose without thorns because she was taught how to take care of everyone else, as opposed to taking care of herself. After the betrayals, hurt, pain and bitterness, she becomes a rose *with* thorns. However, the thorns pricked and scared her, because she was groomed to be what other people wanted her to be. Now she has to learn how to handle the thorns of life on her own.

As the thorns grow thicker and sharper, her personality changes; she is now labeled as bitter, quick-tempered, and a bad influence on others because her attitude has changed. Sad to say, the same people who molded her to be the "perfect" young lady, are the ones who are back-biting her. They fail to realize it was their doing. Everyone should be born with thorns so that they are entitled to make mistakes and learn from them. They will know how it feels to love, to be loved, and to know how to heal if love doesn't work out accordingly.

Most importantly, a little girl should be taught that she should love herself first, flaws (thorns) and all. However, she's been raised as a rose without knowing how to handle the pricks from the thorns. She's left alone to learn how to heal.

A young lady should have the free will to get out of the box and follow her dreams. Leadership is needed to help her live the best life she can live for herself, and let everything else fall into place.

A young lady is taught to never fuss or complain, and to always keep a smile on her face. When a young lady speaks her mind, she is labeled as being impolite and is told to be cautious and mindful of what she says.

Instead of being groomed for her future husband and/or career, a young lady should be first taught to love herself. I am a firm believer that if you put yourself first and find out who you are as a person, everything else will fall into place.

Sadly, that is not what a young lady is taught.

We are taught to love others and to put everyone's needs before our own. We are taught to make sacrifices at an early age to the point where we do not know any better as we age. The edges of our life are rough because we do not know who we are as a person.

After we become a daughter, we become a wife to our husbands and a mother to our children. I believe that is why a woman smiles through the pain because she was always told what she couldn't or shouldn't do. Regardless of this, she believed in herself and made it happen.

It is time to stop molding our girls to please others. It is time to stop teaching our girls that they should bend over backward to make a man feel good about himself. A woman shouldn't ever have to belittle herself to make a man feel as though he is being the man.

It is time to stop a young woman from being manipulated to break her ass and tear herself down to the core in order to build a man up. Once she builds him up, more than half the time he leaves her to figure out the million-piece puzzle of life. Wow! It never amazes me how men forget who was there for them when they didn't have a damn thing to their name. It's timeout for that! Time expired.

It's time to stop allowing people to blame the woman for everything. As women, we try to figure out what they need, what they want; and the entire time we're stressing ourselves out and they don't give a shit as long as it's done. Hell, no. Timeout for that too! We do not give a rat's ass anymore—they are quick to blame us for their mess-ups and think we are supposed to make magic happen. It is time to let them deal with it and figure out how they are going to mend their shit. If they want to blame us, let them, who cares? Their shit isn't our problem.

Go ahead, blame the women. We are holding up the peace sign, smiling and laughing, feeling good as we press forward!

We are free and feel refreshed. It feels good to be the last one standing. We look at life totally differently, and we now see that it's okay to be a little rough around the edges.

It is time for self-fulfillment. Take a deep breath. Tell yourself that you are in love with yourself. You might be asking yourself, what's next? You have to realize that the struggle that was once laid on you wasn't your struggle to carry. We have to realize as women that most of the time the debts that we carry aren't our debts to pay off.

We accumulate other's people debts and make them our own. As we make them our own, their responsibilities fall solely on us. Now is the time to transfer their debt back into their account and let them figure out how they going to pay off their own debt. We, as women, need to realize we are not responsible for other people's debts, only our own, and we will finally see the load will be a lot lighter. We have to stop making life easy for other people. We give them life, yet they take life from us. We want to live, and it starts with self-fulfillment!

We are in a position of power, and it begins by honoring, loving, and putting ourselves first. As we work on the process of accepting ourselves, we have to learn how to train our minds. We are what we think. Be honest with yourself. Write yourself a letter of change and read it to yourself while looking in the mirror. Go to a quiet place and read it to yourself again. If you have to go into a deep silence to learn more about yourself, that's okay.

Know that things will not happen overnight because you are a work in progress. Do not focus on the time, focus on *you*—loving you, learning more about you, and as you work on your internal condition on a daily basis, embrace your inner and outer beauty.

There will be days when you might have a relapse. This is normal. This is when you should not get in your own way. Think positive and write positive affirmations, such as:

1. I'm embracing change for the better.
2. I'm finding comfort in getting to know my weaknesses and my strengths.
3. I am grateful and joyful for the smallest moments.
4. I am crossing the bridges of my fears, and I'm close to reaching my full potential.
5. I am up for the challenge!

Know that you are moving in a positive direction, building security, and discovering a better sense of yourself. When you are going through those stages it is best to take everyone's character at face value. If not, you will be sidetracked, hypnotized, and distracted by their lies. Do not let their toxic energy weigh you down. Your goal is to push out the old cycle so you can focus on your fresh start.

Discipline is key when you're working on self-fulfillment. Therefore, you must stay on course. Success is an 'inside job' because it starts with working on yourself first before you can reap any benefits.

From the honest conversations you are having with yourself you are learning how to be your everything. You know when it is necessary to bite your tongue, and when the battle is worth fighting, or better off being left alone. You've been a work in progress because your bitter days have turned into better days, and great days are ahead as you grow within yourself.

As your inner voice reminds you to treat yourself better, you'll find you're giving yourself an extra push as you determine to give yourself every bit of you, and nothing less. It feels good to know how much you are able to give to yourself rather than others. It feels even better to know that you have molded yourself to never give up on yourself.

You are claiming what is yours, and that is a prosperous life. A prosperous life of peace, joy, love, happiness, inspiration, creativity, hope and guidance. Although it was taken from you because you were brainwashed to put others first, you have found your birthright. Having a prosperous life has always been your birthright!

After you give yourself the chance to get to know yourself, love on yourself, and finally, put yourself first, you'll be like a kid in the candy store because your life is so sweet. This is because you've accepted your flaws, you've learned how to say no without regret, you're giving yourself so much attention and are loving yourself to the moon and back.

You are in your 'Ah-ah' moment, and goodness gracious, you are in the zone where nobody can interrupt your inner peace. As others' houses of cards fall down, you press forward because that isn't your problem. You are taking happy steps, your mind is on cruise control, and you've created a new and improved plan for your life. Life is good!

You're in the process of learning who you are, and you are loving every step. You've moved past needing the approval of others. The counterfeit emotions you once had from their judgment have burned away in the fire.

You are the author of your story, you are the narrative, and you choose to live and enjoy life!

Here and now, you are making a vow to love yourself wholeheartedly. Self-fulfillment is your outer and inner peace. You are loving the change in the wind. You have a sound mind. You are not worried about the things you cannot change. Storms come to clear the air. Your mind is renewed as you gain and fulfill your purpose in life.

Don't be afraid to step out, enjoy, and be free from everyone's worries. It is time to live for yourself without guilt or baggage. Smell the fresh air of freedom. You deserve it!

AFFIRMATION

"Take the needle off the record that keeps playing the same song. A full range of potential is headed your way with new discoveries that are going to take you places you only dreamt of. Instead of dreaming—WAKE UP! It is now your reality."

A Powerful Force

Women can be a powerful force if we come together, as opposed to being hurtful and jealous of each other. There are some women who would rather see another woman down and out and never think to lift a helping hand. There are some women who love to start drama and walk away after they've dropped a toxic bomb without taking responsibility for their actions. Some women are selfish to the point that they will stab another woman in the back to get what they want by any means necessary. The women I dislike the most are the ones you help out and they abuse your kindness and play the victim.

One of my clients called me at the last minute because her CPR Certification was about to expire within a couple of days. She was in a panic because she was afraid she was going to lose her job if she didn't renew her certification. Normally, I do not work with anyone that needs to become certified at the last minute because they already know when their certification is going to expire.

She needed to be certified within two days or she would lose her job. She humbly confessed that she didn't have the money to pay for the certification at the moment. She went on to say she would pay me $80 on the 15th of the month. I trusted her and went out of my way to certify her, and I paid for the card out of my own pocket.

As the 15th was closing in she called me and said, "Charlena, I will not have the money on the 15th. Can I send it to you on the 30th?

I said "Okay."

Time went by and I didn't hear anything from her. I reached out to her several times, but I didn't receive a response. As time moved on, I reached out again and left her a voicemail. She finally contacted me by text and said, "Charlena, I cannot send you the money through Cashapp because it isn't working. May I have your address?"

I replied, "Okay, here is my address."

I never received the payment in the mail. I needed that money because $80 can go a long way when you have to provide for your family.

Weeks later, I sent her a text. I was very upset and told her I couldn't believe that she would be so dishonest. I went on to say that I was going to void her card because I went out of my way to help her; not to mention I paid for the card out of my own pocket.

That got her attention. She responded immediately by text and said, "Are you serious? I can't believe you would think about voiding my card because of $80. You've got to be joking me. It isn't like they will find out where I work."

She sent another text saying, "You are going back and forth with me over $80. This is unbelievable."

She really played the role of the victim; as if I was in the wrong.

I responded, "Yes, I am serious. I did you a favor, and you are working because of my kindness that you took for granted. You took advantage and used me. You could have kept in contact as opposed to disappearing. Better yet, you could have told the truth. Instead, you had one excuse after another. I'm sure you've received three paychecks already, yet you refuse to pay off your debt."

I went on to say, "I didn't have to help you. I helped you from the kindness of my heart. I know now, from my experience with you that I will not ever help anyone in advance. They will have to pay upfront or they will not be able to work. You make it harder for people who are really trying and do not have money at the moment. You are a bad seed and make it more difficult for people who are working hard to make a living. They lose a lot because people do not give them a chance. People like myself build a wall of protection because we have been screwed over by people like you who we tried to help."

She texted me back, saying, "I'm done and not dealing with this anymore."

Later that evening, she called me. I didn't answer.

I texted her and said, "I do not have anything to say. You have the address to send the funds for the card. You can also use Cashapp for a faster transaction. Other than that, I do not have anything to say."

I was so angry. I told her I should take her to court and make her pay for my court fees on top of the $80 she owed me.

I didn't take her to court; nor did I void her card.

Weeks passed and the issue still wasn't settled. I sent her messages to her email, WhatsApp, and her phone; I knew she was going to get one of the three.

I said, "I notice I haven't received your payment of $80 in the mail. Please be fair and send the payment by Cashapp. I work hard to make a living for myself and my three children; I'm sure you can relate to that. I did not report your card because I know you have to work and make a living, just as I have to work to make a living and provide for my children and myself. I am a fair and good person. Are you going to send your payment? Nowadays, $80 goes a long way. I need that $80. It could help put food in my children's mouths and/or pay a bill. I work hard to earn every penny I make. I also try to help people like you in the process. Please be a decent human being. I helped you out when you needed your card to continue to work, and I was honest with you. Thank you."

Needless to say, I didn't hear anything from her after I sent the messages. One thing's for sure, I now know people mess up a good thing for others. I felt used, and I won't ever allow myself to feel that way again. Feeling used from helping someone is an awful feeling; it made me feel defeated because there wasn't anything I could do about it.

I wonder how some individuals can use people and not have any remorse. They walk around freely without a care in the world.

I was a caring woman helping another woman because I wanted her to get ahead and stay ahead. What made matters worse in my opinion, is the fact that she has a family as well, so she should have known I needed every penny to provide for my family.

I helped her because I remember when I was down on my luck when my husband left and I had to make a choice to either pay the gas, water, electric bill or put gas in my car. The children couldn't miss school, so I decided to put gas in my car for the next two weeks.

I went to different organizations to see if someone could help me pay my utility bills. There were about eight or nine of them that told me no because all of the bills were in my husband's name. They calmly told me that they would like to help, but they had to follow protocol. I understood. However, I needed to be given a chance. I needed help.

I went to an organization called Zion Hill in East Point, Georgia. An older lady told me she couldn't help me. I told her I understood, and that she was the tenth person who'd said they couldn't help.

As I walked out the door, she stopped me and said, "Let me see what I can do." In order for her to help me, I had to take classes through their organization for them to pay the bill. I was grateful! However, I was wondering, *how in the world will I be able to attend these classes?*

At that time, I was attending two schools because I'd lost my financial aid. I was receiving aid at one school because I took on a full load, and paying for my classes at the previous school I was attending so I could graduate. I thought to myself that attending three different locations for classes was impossible. I needed assistance to pay a bill. She gave me a chance; therefore, I had to make it work.

Although Zion Hill was going to pay for one bill, I needed assistance to pay the remaining bills for the month. I called around, but again, everyone said they couldn't help. The Great Divine led me to Ebenezer Baptist Church. I sat in their parking lot as I looked up their phone number. I called, and an older lady answered the phone. I told her about my situation and she asked me to bring all the bills I needed help with and she would see what she could do.

I walked up to the church, and as I rang the doorbell an older lady dressed in all white, with gray hair, was waiting by the door.

She opened the door, smiled, and said, "Hello."

I smiled back, looked down slightly in shame. As I looked up, I said,

"Hello, how are you doing?"

She looked at me and said, "There's no need to be ashamed. I'm here to help you if I can."

I smiled at her, and this time I didn't look down.

"How can I help you? Are you the young lady who was on the phone a couple of minutes ago?" she asked.

"Yes. I am Charlena," I said as I held my hand out to shake her hand.

The entire time she was smiling as she said, "Let me see your bills, sweetie."

As I handed them over, she said, "Your mother gave you a manly name. I thought you said your name is Charlena."

I laughed and said, "Yes, ma'am. My name is Charlena. The name on my bills is my husband's name."

She smiled and said, "Oh, I see."

She added up the bills, including the electricity bill.

I said, "Ma'am, you do not have to put in the electricity bill; an organization is helping me pay that one."

She said, "I am going to write a check out for it anyway because you are going to need it; it's cold outside. Use the check they give you to pay for it next month."

I asked, "Ma'am, are you sure? I do not want to take money from someone else who needs help."

She touched my hand and said, "Charlena, I am positive."

She wrote each name of the utility companies on separate checks and the amount owing.

She smiled and said, "It's after 5 p.m. Make sure you pay your bills first thing in the morning."

I smiled and said, "Yes, Ma'am, I will. Thank you so much!"

She stepped forward to give me a hug and said, "Charlena, it might be hard now, but you are learning, growing, and you are going to change the world in ways you never knew. Take advantage and let God use you according to His will. Remember these trying times and tell the world so you can help others see there is a way, and anything is possible."

I cried on her shoulder. I apologized for wetting her white dress. She put her hands on my cheeks and said, "Charlena, you are going to be okay."

After I pulled up in my driveway and walked into the house, it was ice cold. I flicked the light switch and the lights were off. I had my headlights and a little light from the street lights to help me gather my children's things.

I stayed the night over at my mother's and cried all night. I held on to what the sweet older lady told me. As I cried my eyes out, I was wondering, *how was God going to use me during my weakest moment?*

I knew how it felt for someone to *not* give you a chance. I also knew how it felt for someone to *give* you a chance. I was blessed and grateful. I didn't take anyone for granted. Zion Hill wrote out a check to my electric company and I held up my end of the deal; I completed the classes. I was tired, but I completed the classes because I was beyond grateful that they gave me a chance and helped me.

It is sad that people like the woman I helped steal other people's chances of becoming a better person. A little help can go a long way. When we help each other, that is a powerful force because everyone wins and the world becomes a better place.

It never fails to amaze me how some women are always trying to compete with you. Or they try to hold you back from what you've worked so hard for. I had an interview at a well-known HBCU school. I felt like, wow, my hard work paid off and this is my chance to help other young girls bloom from being princesses to queens!

The Human Resource Department was kind and the receptionist in the Department of Physical Education was very polite and kind as well. We had a great conversation as if we knew each other from past lives.

As my name was called, she wished me the best of luck! I smiled and said, "Thank you kindly."

During the interview, it was all females; and everyone seemed to be very welcoming.

One young lady around my age, maybe a little older by some years, looked at me with a straight face and said, "Okay, let's get started. Charlena, describe yourself."

Although I have a lot to say about myself, and I can talk about myself all day, I took the proper route—I didn't want to talk too much. Therefore, I described myself in a short, yet, professional way.

The director had her hand on her chin and said, "Impressive."

I smiled and said, "Thank you."

The director wrote some notes in her black agenda and said, "Charlena, how do you keep up with your daily schedule and activities?"

I replied, "I program everything into my phone and it automatically transfers to my calendar in my email address."

The director laughed and said, "I see that you are an honest person."

I replied, "Yes, ma'am. I am not perfect, but I try to be."

As she continued to laugh, she said, "You tickled me because you are the first person that said you used your phone. Little does everyone know, I use my phone as well. Everyone I've interviewed so far said they have a black book and other things they used to use back in the day before technology became so advanced. Thank you, Charlena, for your honesty."

She smiled and said, "You've made my day! Finally, someone telling the truth for once."

I replied, "You're welcome."

After the interview, the lady who was a few years older than me, walked me out. As she showed me to the door she said, "I noticed the director really gravitated towards you, which isn't common. I've been working here for years, and I'll be damned if I let someone of your caliber come and take my spot."

I was taken back because I didn't see that dark turn coming. I looked at her and politely said, "I understand you are the manager of the Wellness Center, and I noticed you have a Bachelor's degree, which is great. However, if you want to keep your "spot" I hope that you are aware that you are not the common dominator. From what I have seen online, everyone that is on the roster has their Masters. From a sister to another sister who wants to help you, I suggest you upgrade your education and earn your Master's degree."

I stepped up a little closer so that nobody would hear our conversation and said, "Wise advice, if you think someone is going to "take" your place; that means you didn't earn it. Nobody can take what you've earned. If I do not earn the position, that means it wasn't for me. However, you need to be cautious because someone is coming in to earn your spot, no matter how you try to sabotage them. They will have more education and more experience than you do. If you don't already know, education talks and experience speaks even louder. Think about that and soak it in like a sponge, because life will show you better than it can tell you."

I didn't get the position, but that was okay because it would have been hell working with her. I wondered, *did she tell everyone who had an interview the same thing, or was it just me?* I looked on the website to see if they filled the position. It said 'position open until filled.' However, I noticed that she no longer worked there.

If women work together instead of trying to hurt or compete against each other, we most definitely will be a powerful force. We have to be open-minded and realize that if we come together and do the unexpected, everything will work together for good. Not only will it work together for good, but we will be strong warriors from the side effects that tried to weaken our inner peace of mind.

If we, as women, embrace each other we will be unstoppable. We must stand together and be counted as one.

As one we are strong.

As one we are tough.

As one we can challenge what the future holds.

As one we are survivors.

As one we have unbelievable courage.

As one we can face any obstacle.

As one we are centered and balanced.

As one we will transform the world.

As one we are pioneers and trailblazers.

As one our opportunities are endless.

We have to realize that we are a powerful force. If we work together, we can make a huge difference in the world, despite our race or religion. If we, as women, dare to come together we can help each other conquer our fears. We can help each other become wiser by teaching and learning from each other.

We need to lift each other up more. Reach down to lend a helping hand. Reach up and tell your sisters of all races and religions, "I am here for you."

After all of the sacrifices we've made for others, surely, we can make sacrifices for each other. As much as we women have loved and (most definitely) lost due to heartbreak, being unappreciated, and working hard on a daily basis, why do we put each other down? Why do we use each other? What is the point of competing? Don't we have enough going against us as it is? We should be able to come together and love one another. We should be able to help each other recover from our losses. That is what I call a powerful force.

A powerful force of women does not have a race or religion. We are human—a powerful human force!

AFFIRMATION

"If women come together, we will be the answer to perfect harmony."

Trailblazers

Your life as a Trailblazer begins at the limit of your comfort zone. The road you've traveled had many detours and delays. However, you paid close attention, as each detour consisted of many uphill battles. As the twisted road caused numerous delays, it triggered confusion as it interrupted your peace and shook your confidence by its unpredictable curves.

You had the choice to give in and remain silent or to never see a problem as a challenge you couldn't overcome. You didn't fear failure; instead, you used your fear to fuel your fire. With each step you made you knew the meaning of balance and patience, and you were wise enough to know you couldn't afford to skip any steps, for each step made a difference in your growth and change.

Trailblazer, you tore down walls of setbacks, let-downs, and rejections, and strengthened your core as you cut the weeds of negative thinking from other people and yourself. Your tears watered and cleansed your mind, body, and soul. This gave you the ability to look deep within yourself to ask yourself the hard, tough, and truthful questions.

Ask yourself the questions that are right for you—that only you can answer truthfully. Do not shortchange yourself. It is time to dissect your mind, your inner thoughts, and secrets. Do not hold anything back from yourself. You have the answers to your questions.

There have been many wars a Trailblazer fought against themselves and others without weapons. However, you created a thicker skin as you let yourself and other people tear your confidence apart. Trailblazer, know that you cannot be your own worst enemy; you are your own strength. If you do not believe in yourself, who will? We all fall short many times, but when we get back up, we must dust ourselves off and charge! Your foundation is solid and it is getting stronger every single day.

Other people's actions gave you a head start because you recognized the red flags and knew that wasn't the right way to go. The force of awareness broadened your vision; you had the keen insight of an eagle. You knew when to soar in the sky with ease and peace. You also knew when to suit up as you looked down and hunted for your prey. The best part of it all was, just as they thought they'd got the best of you, you attacked at the right time, and they never saw it coming.

Trailblazer, you are a warrior! At times, are you underestimated? At times you are called the weakest link. There were so many sacrifices you made, and afterward, you felt like pure shit. The resentment pulled and spread like mold, and the mold's side effects made you sick and disgusted from loving so hard and losing so much. The ripple effects crossed each other as they manipulated your mind to think negative thoughts. However, the ripple effects also opened your heart to feel and know how to love yourself. As you started your journey of self-fulfillment, all the hell you've been through changed you from a fallen warrior into a fearless powerful force with fabulous potential!

There were many pioneers who came before you that also felt a sense of hopelessness. They were judged because they were women. At times they felt helpless but that didn't stop them from making their mark as they made changes in the world which people thought were impossible. They made themselves into believers because of their accomplishments.

These pioneers did not have the technology and resources that we have today. However, they used what they were given, which was their God-given talent. "We will be heard, seen, and we are untouchable." The pioneer's voices were rising louder, stronger, and their voices were heard as they made the impossible, possible.

Their mentality was, "We will not be ignored. We are human and we should be treated equally, just like men." As they rose to the challenges they endured, their great strength of determination spoke without the need for words.

Our pioneers gave us a head start. They prepared us to fight many battles for decades to come as they left the map for us to continue on the path of their greatness. As quoted by the great Susan B. Anthony, *"Oh, if I could but live another century and see the fruition of all the work for women! There is so much yet to be done."*

The shade of our skin might be a bit darker or lighter, but we share the same rejections and discriminations as we are treated unfairly because we are women. Our religions might very well be different; however, we share the same identity, being females productively working for change for a greater cause.

As women, we have come a long way but the struggle is real and our hunger is stirring up the right to be treated equally regardless of age, religion, race, and or which "group" we belong to. There is so much more that needs to be done, but if we continue to come together as women instead of being each other's enemies, filled with the rage of envy and competition, we will be able to move further along a lot faster than expected.

We have to take up the cross that was left by our Pioneers; they got us as far as they could. It is now our time to take advantage of the tools that were left for us and open the doors of our opportunities as women. We have to lead by example for our little girls and young ladies who will soon take up the torch. We have to show them by our actions that women's opportunities are never-ending. Their assumptions must not take us off-course because our minds are too sharp and powerful to dwell on their insecurities, and we do not have time to stray off track.

When a woman is passive, it is acceptable. However, when a woman speaks her mind and voices her opinion, that is a serious problem. A woman's voice should count, but sadly, when a woman speaks, people hear only what they want to hear; the rest falls on deaf ears. When things do not work out as planned, a woman has to step up to the plate to fix the problem that she had a solution for in the first place.

When a woman is independent, that's also a huge issue. I have noticed that an independent woman is spoken down to because she is fearless, free, and she would rather walk alone because she knows her worth. Ladies, there is nothing wrong with that!

We are Trailblazers!

Our Shero's used their brains to spark the flame.

We, as women, have to learn we cannot always do everything alone; coming together as one produces greatness as we lay the foundation together.

All women are Trailblazers who've put in the work, and as we all know, nothing comes easy. Therefore, the time and hard work we've invested is ours that we earned; because it most definitely wasn't given.

Trailblazers, we must own our lives, filter out what doesn't serve us, and stand firm for what we believe in.

Our voices are beautiful and powerful!

Our minds are creative and knowledgeable.

Yet time and time again, our needs and wants fell on deaf ears. We were told we weren't good enough. We were abused mentally, physically, and emotionally. We were told with nasty sarcastic remarks at times, and here and there may be a laugh that made the insult worse; "It would be your word against mine, and guess who they are going believe? Not you."

One by one we took a chance to speak up, but our voices weren't heard. They tried to make us feel threatened; as if we were going to lay down and be stepped on like shit on the bottom of their shoe. We interrupted their comfort zone and showed them their time was up!

Their time of talking and belittling us this way has expired. They tried, but they failed to realize we are strong and we will never give up.

Their time of thinking they can touch us inappropriately and we will keep quiet has expired. No! We will rise up and bring the world to its feet. Trust me… We will be seen and heard!

Their time of trying to break us down has expired. No! We can move mountains!

Their time of pointing their fingers at us and putting F.E.A.R (False Evidence Appearing Real) into our minds by making us believe it is our fault has expired. No! It is not our fault. It never was!

Their time of nasty insults has expired.

Their time of preying off vulnerable women who have to "make a deal" to get a higher position they earned has expired. No! Your "man"ipulation has no effect. We, as women, have full ownership of our minds, bodies, and souls.

Why should a woman tear herself down to make a man feel like a man? Ladies, it is not our duty to feed a man's ego and to curb his insecurities.

I admire so many women who are stepping up, coming forth and speaking their truth. I am so inspired because our young ladies are following our lead. They are taking a stand and laying the foundation for little girls in the future.

We made it clear by movements such as MeToo and Times Up, that we are not bowing down and keeping quiet anymore. Together we are the movement! Together we are one! Together we will make a significant change! There are no ifs ands or buts about it. We are not lacking anything, because as women we can always create something from nothing.

Ladies, it is time to take back what's been ours all along. We, as women, are the backbone that keeps the world turning. We are the voices that *will* be respected. Each step we make *will* forever be remembered. We are here to empower each other as we walk through this journey we call life together.

We shouldn't let anyone or anything divide us because as one, we are a powerful source. We are the common denominator; it is in our flesh, blood, and soul. We have a fire under our feet. Each step we take is carving out the path for our young ladies who follow, and we must remember that we need to practice self-acceptance and self-love.

No, you are not perfect. What's important is that you know your self-worth and you are happy; and that's all that matters. You now know that you should never underestimate your ability to create your own happiness.

Loving yourself first is the foundation that you should never take for granted.

Embrace your individuality by embracing your authentic self. Go deeper to develop a relationship with yourself. Accept who you are; because self-love requires discipline. Create a life that you know is yours—the key to a better you is perseverance.

It is okay to ask for a helping hand, for we will be standing together when all is said and done.

Do not connect your self-worth to the thoughts or words of others. Don't worry about other's opinions of you. Who cares? Be brave and do not be ashamed to dance to the beat of your own drum because it is impossible to please others.

Your story has changed from disappointment to achievement. You've changed the script to love yourself, therefore, love, love, and love yourself more. Accumulate self-love; raise your expectations; value your characteristics, and most importantly, love yourself wholeheartedly.

Happiness is precious.

Happiness is courage.

Happiness is patience.

Happiness is never giving up on your dreams. They told me that I would never get to tell my story but I am stronger than I knew. Their voices were poison. I wasn't going to let them steal my joy. There was no way in hell I was going to let them write my beginning or end. The chapters in my life are going to be told by the person who lived it, and that's me.

They want to see us fall apart but that isn't possible. They think they have broken us and shattered us into pieces but because of our thick skin, we are able to walk through fire.

Our roots run deep and are strong to the core. As the saying goes, what does not kill us makes us stronger. There is no compromising when they try to make us the victim; our inner strength gives us the courage to know that way deep down inside, we are victorious.

I am proud to see women taking a stand. Many times, we have been fallen warriors; there have been plenty of times we have been wounded warriors, but we are still standing. We are standing up for our rights. We are standing up for a cause. We are standing up for movements that empower us to be heard, respected and appreciated!

We are bold!

We are courageous!

We are thankful!

We are grateful!

We are blessed!

Our Pioneers and Trailblazers who dared to make the journey into the unknown have given us the courage to break out of our comfort zone to dare to be unique, magnificent, phenomenal; and have set ideals to stand for the power of truth.

Ruth Bader Ginsburg Lawyer and Associate Justice of the U.S. Supreme Court.

"My mother told me to be a lady. And for her, that meant to be your own person, be independent."

"Women will only have true equality when men share with them the responsibility of bringing up the next generation."

"The state controlling a woman would mean denying her full autonomy and full equality."

Harriet Tubman (the Moses of her people) was enslaved, escaped, and helped others gain their freedom as a "conductor" of the Underground Railroad.

"Every great dream begins with a dreamer. Always remember, you have within you the strength, the patience, and the passion to reach for the stars to change the world."

Elizabeth Cady Stanton was an American suffragist, social activist, abolitionist, and a leading figure in the early women's rights movement.

"We hold these truths to be self-evident: that all men and women are created equal.
The best protection any woman can have... is courage."

Susan B. Anthony was an American social reformer and women's rights activist who played a pivotal role in the women's suffrage movement.

"I declare to you that woman must not depend upon the protection of man, but must be taught to protect herself, and there I take my stand."

Elizabeth Blackwell was the first woman to graduate from medical school in the United States.

"I do not wish to give (women) a first place, still less a second one—but the complete freedom to take their true place, whatever it may be."

Fanny Jackson Coppin African-American who became one of the first black women to earn a college degree. Educator, missionary and a lifelong advocate for female higher education.

"There is too much repression and suppression in schools."

Gabrielle Bonheur "Coco" Chanel was a French fashion designer; and the founder of the Chanel brand.

"In order to be irreplaceable, one must always be different."

Eleanor Roosevelt was the longest-serving First Lady of the United States. She proved that the FLOTUS office could be a position of influence on the nation.

"Women are like teabags. You don't know how strong they are until you put them into hot water."

Marie Curie was a French Physicist. She was the first woman to win a Nobel Prize in Physics. Furthermore, she earned a Nobel Prize in Chemistry. She became the first person to claim Nobel honors twice.

"One never notices what has been done; one can only see what remains to be done."

Sarah Breedlove (Madam C. J. Walker) created hair products for American-American hair. She was the first American woman to become a self-made millionaire.

"I am a woman who came from the cotton fields of the South. From there I was promoted to the washtub. From there I was promoted to the cook kitchen. And from there I promoted myself into the business of manufacturing hair goods and preparations... I have built my own factory on my own ground."

Amelia Earhart was the first female pilot to fly across the Atlantic Ocean.

"The woman who can create her own job is the woman who will win fame and fortune."

Rosa Louise McCauley Parks was an activist in the civil rights movement best known for taking a stand. (Montgomery Bus Boycott).

"No, the only tired I was, was tired of giving in."

Shirley Chisholm was the first black woman elected to the United States Congress as she represented New York's 12th Congressional District for seven terms from 1968-1983. She became the first black candidate to make a bid for the U.S. presidency.

"The emotional, sexual, and psychological stereotyping of females begins when

the doctor says, "It's a girl."

Coretta Scott King helped lead the Civil Rights Movement in the 1960s. She also was a front and center advocate for African-American equality.

"The woman power of this nation can be the power which makes us whole and heals the rotten community, now so shattered by war and poverty and racism. I have great faith in the power of women who will dedicate themselves wholeheartedly to the task of remaking our society."

Patsy Mink the first woman of color elected to Congress; and the first Asian American in the House. She became a politician, advocated tirelessly for Title IX, and transformed the educational opportunities available to millions of American women.

"We have to build things that we want to see accomplished, in life and in our country, based on our own personal experiences…to make sure that others… do not have to suffer the same discrimination."

Sandra Day O'Connor was the first woman appointed and served 24 years in the U.S. Supreme Court.

"The more education a woman has, the wider the gap between men's and women's earnings for the same work."

Sally Kristen Ride In 1983 she became the first American woman in space.

"The stars don't look bigger, but they do look brighter."

Condoleezza Rice is the first black woman to serve as the United States' National Security Advisor. 2005-2009 she was the first black woman to serve as U.S. Secretary of State.

"The day has to come when it's not a surprise that a woman has a powerful position."

Mae C. Jemison In 1992 she was aboard the Space Shuttle Endeavour as the first African-American female astronaut in space.

"What we find is that if you have a goal that is very, very, far out, and you approach it in little steps, you start to get there faster. Your mind opens up to the possibilities."

J.K. Rowling is the first self-made billionaire author in history.

"Anything's possible if you've enough nerve."

Halle Berry The first African-American woman to win an Academy Award for Best Actress.

"I think it's always best to be who you are."

Tarana Burke is an African-American civil rights activist who founded the MeToo movement.

"If we're ever going to heal in our community, we have to heal the perpetrators and heal the survivors, or else it's just a continuous cycle."

Rachel Morrison The first African-American woman in nine decades to receive an Academy Award Oscar nomination for cinematography.

"You just sort of get used to being one of the only women on set, so it's really refreshing to start to enter a time when that's not the case anymore."

Ibtihaj Muhammad became the first Muslim-American woman to win a bronze medal for the United States at the Rio Olympic Games.

"Even if we're facing bigotry or racism, we can still be successful."

Gabby Douglas is the first African-American to win the individual all-around and team events at the 2012 London Olympics games.

"Always be courageous and strong, and don't fear."

Malala Yousafzai is an advocate and spokesperson for girls' education. In 2014, she was the youngest person to earn the Nobel Peace Prize.

"If one man can destroy everything, why can't one girl change it?"

AFFIRMATION

"Groundbreaker! Stomp the ground and make your mark."

Affirmations

*"Wake up! Become more aware and alive of what feeds **YOUR** soul without seeking permission from others. Many curve balls have been thrown. Don't hesitate—NOW is the time to hit a home run."*

"Ladies, it's harvest time!!! Take care of your crops,
water them and weed them out."

*"Don't bury yourself in broken dreams of resentment.
Expand your life purpose and reap the benefit of happiness!"*

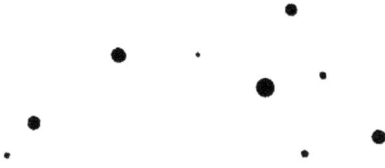

"Take the healing that is being offered. Untangle your fears. Confidence and perseverance are your purposes."

"Another one bites the dust. I am reaping the benefit of self-fulfillment and self-control. I am worthy of all the good things in life."

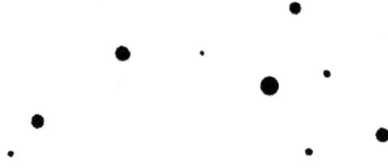

"Queen! You are powerful! Act like you know it!"

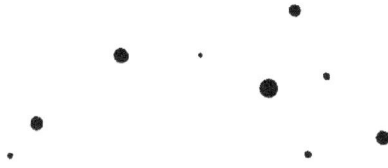

"No more brainwashing—expect the unexpected to blow your mind! Connect with yourself and your life's purpose—then grow."

"Take the needle off the record that keeps playing the same song. A full range of potential is headed your way with new discoveries that are going to take you places you only dreamt of. Instead, of dreaming—WAKE UP! It is now your reality."

"If women come together, we will be the answer to perfect harmony."

"Groundbreaker! Stomp the ground and make your mark."

Introduction for the book:
I'm Speaking Up but You're Not Listening 2nd edition

We want to protect our children by any means necessary. Sadly, we cannot be with them every moment of the day. I never thought I would have to teach my children to defend themselves at such a young age. Children are supposed to be free spirits, dream chasers, and thinking of limitless opportunities. They are supposed to be filled with light that shines with happiness and joy that shouldn't be dimmed or filled with darkness and fear.

Children should be living carefree lives and always smiling, laughing, filled with peace, and harmony; not worrying about the troubles of what tomorrow may bring. Our children should have a wide range of imagination and think about the greatest achievements that they want to accomplish; not making sacrifices by having to give up their clothes, lunch money, or being robbed of their personality, and stripped of their self-esteem.

As parents, guardians, teachers, and school administrators, we should be giving our children better days, we are the outcome of their future, we are the pieces of the puzzle – pieces that restore their shattered confidence. When our children are hopeless, we are the light that shines brightly to renew their hope. Our love and actions are the hope that floats to restore what was lost and to renew strength that they never imagined existed.

We are our children's voices when all else has failed. As parents, guardians, teachers, and school administrators, we have to be more involved in our children's lives. Bullying shouldn't be taken lightly. However, it's a sad fact that bullying is played down in schools by some teachers, administrators, and sometimes at home by the parents.

We have to change this continuous cycle. It has gone on too far for way too long. Our children shouldn't be victims of suicide or have suicidal thoughts because someone thinks they have the ability to strip them bit by bit and piece by piece of their birthright of life.

We must fight for our children; our voices are louder and the roar of our demand for change will be heard loud and clear. We will burn the ashes of fear from our children because we are a source of empowerment.

Our children are special, they are unique, they are a gift, and they are our children that we love dearly. Without a doubt, change will come and we must make that change happen because bullying is not accepted.

We shouldn't give anyone the ability to rob our children of happiness. We have the power to change the situation. For those who feel as though bullying is an unknown situation, let's dare to be different and make the situation known by opening the problem at hand by speaking up and finding a solution to the problem. We should always remember, when a problem occurs, we must not forget that there's always a solution.

Now is the time to decide to make the change. Now is the time to dissect and look at every angle in the distasteful world of bullying. Now is the time for us to put our best foot forward and take on the responsibility of saving our children from being killed or destroyed by bullying; also, known as the Silent Killer. Our children shouldn't be prisoners of what a bully has cast on them. Our children want their voices to be heard; and as the adults in charge, our voices will be heard.

The time has come to take action to stop bullying – and the time is now!

Introduction for the book:
Dear Fathers of the Fatherless Children

The choices we make in life can make or break us. However, some people make choices out of selfish reasons; not knowing their actions at the present time will have repercussions in the future. We are told not to worry about tomorrow; for tomorrow is not promised. That could be very well true. However, what if tomorrow *is* promised; how would you reexamine yesterday? What would you do differently today? How would you prepare for tomorrow?

We are told to live for today, however, the question is—how many people live for "today?" If you are living for "today" at the end of the day, could you say you took care of all of your responsibilities? Each day has a purpose; each day creates a memory, and each day should be precious.

Ask yourself—did you put your best foot forward? Or did you point fingers at everyone else instead of focusing on what you need to improve? The important question is: at the end of each day are you satisfied with the decisions you've made?

Dear Fathers of the Fatherless Children:

Do you know your sons and daughters are AMAZING? They are full of life and they are truly a blessing. Your sons and daughters need you in their lives. How is it possible that at the beginning of the day when you open your eyes, your children are not on your priority list? Fathers of the fatherless children, your sons and daughters crave your presence and your support. They want you in their lives more than you will ever know. There isn't such a thing as a part-time father; your children shouldn't be treated as toys that you can throw in the closet when you are tired or when the going gets rough. Your sons and daughters are human; they should feel loved and nothing less at all times. You say you love your children, but actions speak louder than words; stand up and be a father to your sons and daughters.

Fathers of the fatherless children, open your eyes and know your presence is very critical. Be your son's hero and let him know he can conquer the world. Be your daughter's first knight in shining armor. Be a part of your son's and daughter's success instead of their pain.

Introduction for the book:
No Cross, No Crown: Trust God Through the Battle 2nd edition

"For I know the plans I have for you," declares the LORD, "Plans to prosper you and not to harm you, plans to give you hope and a future" (Jeremiah 29:11).

Life is full of surprises. We find ourselves free-falling as we love freely; rejoicing in giving and not looking for anything in return; smiling without expecting to grieve; laughing not knowing pain is right around the corner. When clouds begin to block the sunlight and the storm is on the way, we move toward shelter because we know that when it rains, it pours. When rain destroys the life we have built, it is hard for some of us to start over. We may think to start over is a bad thing; however, we never take time out to have a clear understanding of why the rain took its course. We begin to think the worst of a bad situation because the thunder shook our confidence, the lightning struck our fears into action, the rain flooded our happiness, and the clouds clouded our train of thought to the point we cannot think clearly.

Sometimes we find ourselves headed down a one-way street; sooner or later we have to make a decision to turn left or right. We need to take the right steps, and use the advantage of the clouds so we can see clearly because the sun can be too bright and hinder our ability to see. That is when we have to step back, reevaluate our life, and understand the meaning of No Cross No Crown.

About the Author

Charlena E. Jackson, B.S., M.S., M.H.A. is a professor at a university in Georgia. She is a prolific writer and has published several books, among them, being: *No Cross, No Crown: Trust God Through the Battle (1st & 2nd edition)*, *Teachers Just Don't Understand Bullying Hurts (1st & 2nd edition)*, *I'm Speaking Up but You're Not Listening (1st & 2nd edition)*, *A Woman's Love is Never Good Enough (1st & 2nd edition)*, *Dear Fathers of the Fatherless Children*, *Dying on the Inside and Suffocating on the Outside*, *and Unapologetic for My Flaws and All (1st and 2nd edition)*. Her positive, dedicated, and determined attitude has encouraged many people to put up a good fight for justice and to be treated with respect. She is currently working on her Ph.D. in Healthcare Administration. Charlena is a much-loved inspirational speaker. She loves to read, roller skate, cycle, write, and travel.

www.ingramcontent.com/pod-product-compliance
Lightning Source LLC
LaVergne TN
LVHW041223080426
835508LV00011B/1052